PEASANT'S CHOICE

More of the Best from

THE URBAN PEASANT

JAMES BARBER

Recipes from the Popular Television Cooking Series

HASTINGS HOUSE · BOOK PUBLISHERS

Mamaroneck, New York

Acknowledgements

PHOTOGRAPHY · *John Sherlock*

PHOTOGRAPHER'S ASSISTANT · *Robert Wright*

FOOD STYLIST · *Nathan Fong*

PRODUCTION MANAGER · *Romney Grant*

PRODUCTION COORDINATOR · *Nancy Briant*

PROJECT EDITOR · *Elizabeth McLean*

Library of Congress Catalog Card Number 94-072929

ISBN 0-8038-9370-1

Published by agreement with Urban Peasant Productions, Ltd.

10 9 8 7 6 5 4 3 2 1

Table of Contents

JAMES BARBER'S passion for food is matched only by his passion for life. Television host of the internationally popular cooking show, *The Urban Peasant*, he is—or has been variously described as—a physicist, engineer, soldier, sailor, miner, journalist, author, actor, grandfather, biker, multilingual world traveller, songwriter and cook. Among many other things, James' boundless energy has resulted in 6 cookbooks preceding *Peasant's Choice*—*Ginger Tea Makes Friends*, *Flash in the Pan*, *Fear of Frying*, and *The Immodest but Honest Good Eating Cookbook*. *The Urban Peasant, More Than a Cookbook* and *The Urban Peasant, Quick and Simple* are companion books to the television series.

Cookbooks, like apples, onions and just about everything else that grows (including you, me and our kids), come in a lot of different shapes and sizes. And like us, some work and some don't. ■ All kids are not the same, although each and every one of them is, to someone, at some time, the very best kid on earth. And every cookbook, at the moment of purchase, is the very best. Maybe it's a birthday present for someone special, and maybe it's just a book for you, perhaps the only cookbook you ever saw that had 27 recipes for chocolate chip cookies all made with garlic and leftover mashed pota-

toes, that being the period in your life when your horoscope said that chocolate and garlic, in alignment, would cause your love life to improve drastically. ■ All good religions celebrate with food, and all good families regularly sit down round a table. Lovers have dinner first, and then they graduate to breakfast. Businessmen eat lunch together, and the very littlest of kids knows the importance of dinner with Grandma. But somehow we've managed to complicate it. Gourmet dinners for company, but "the usual" all week. And the usual is usually much more boring than it has to be.

■ There are too many gourmets, too many fancy ingredients, too many one-purpose pots and pans and too many of those beautiful photographs that make the average cook feel incompetent. Cooking ought to be fun, it ought to be easy, and it ought to be something we can all do, and enjoy, together. ■ Dinner didn't ought to be a Broadway show, with weeks of rehearsals and critics passing judgement on opening night. It's not romantic to say that the best ingredient is love—it's just true. ■ A little bit of care, a little bit of pride, and a little bit of self-confidence. ■ We buy cookbooks in moments of passion. We want them to bring pleasure and give pleasure, along with joy and happiness and most usually, togetherness. I hope this book is going to do all of those things, but most of all I want it to make cooking easy, and quick. ■ I'd like to know that a lot of mothers got breakfast in bed because of this book. I'd like a lot of guys to discover how easy it is to make dinner, and a lot of students to find that they can get through university without their mothers or Chinese takeout. ■ Most of all, I'd like to know that a lot of people are going to have a lot of fun with this book. There's not much in it you can't buy in the corner store, nothing you need a degree in modern languages to understand. It's easy. Dead easy. ■

Snacks &
Appetizers

A snack is a snack, nothing more, nothing less. You're hungry, you eat. Before dinner, before bed. Some eat carrots, some eat cookies, some eat potato chips or chocolate bars, and some, let's face it, eat themselves into a larger waist size every month. ■ There's nothing really wrong with snacks—our bodies are telling us they need something, and we're doing the best we can to listen. But we've managed to turn anything other than a fully balanced meal into a life-threatening sin. And sin, as we all know, is attractive, just because it is a sin. ■ Junk food is easy, it's available, it's usually pretty (if you're into packages), so, one bite at a time, we get into junk food. Which, in large quantities, is indeed life-threatening, first because it stops us thinking about what our bodies really need, and second, even more important, it takes advantage of our inbred fears about trying anything different. ■ But if we'd stop listening all the time to the doom and gloomers, stop worrying about the food rules, we'd probably be a lot looser in what we chose to eat. There's no point in continually worrying about whether you should use 1 or 2 tablespoons of cooking oil when, suddenly, to compensate for all that worry you're going to go out and wolf down the half cup of saturated fat that is in a large pack of potato chips. And then feel guilty. ■ The good news is, it's time to dump the guilt. Medical science has decided that we no longer have to punish ourselves to feel good. Cravings are normal, cravings are part of who we are, and their best advice is "Don't fight it." The theory works like this: cravings are your body's way of making sure that we have the energy we need to carry on living and working and breeding. The secret is to figure out the *kind* of food your body craves (starch, protein, or energy foods like sugar and fat) and recognize that your body wants it because it needs it. Then find reasonably healthy versions of these things and go ahead and snack on them during the day. It's as simple as drinking when you're thirsty. Give your body what it needs, and if you still have the odd unhealthy craving—go ahead and indulge it, guilt-free. Finally the diet gurus have come up with a theory that the rest of us would call "common sense." ■ "OK," you say, "but is it still a sin for me, if I want to be a good cook, to even think about French fries?" And the answer is that it's perfectly okay for you to think of anything, provided it gives you pleasure, because that pleasure, if you really savour it, is going to make you even more appreciative of everything else you eat. But if you sneak out to McDonald's, hide in the bushes so no one can see you, and scoff them down on full automatic, you're never going to be a better cook, or a better eater, or thinner, or less of a couch potato. ■

Empanadas

(em-pah-**nah**-thas)

Don't be scared of making your own pastry. Just remember two things. The more you handle the dough the tougher it becomes, so work quickly and lightly using either your fingertips, a pastry cutter or a food processor. And have all your utensils and ingredients as cool as possible. Then just get on and enjoy it. But if you're in a hurry (which many restaurant cooks are) use store-bought pastry.

PASTRY

¼ cup/50 mL butter
1 tsp/5 mL baking powder
2 egg yolks (reserve one for later)

1 cup/250 mL flour
½ tsp/2.5 mL salt
4 Tbsp/60 mL ice-cold water

Cube the butter and put into a food processor with the flour, baking powder and salt. Pulse for about half a minute or until the mixture resembles coarse breadcrumbs. Add one egg yolk and pulse again. Add the water one spoon at a time until the dough comes away in a ball.

If working by hand, work the butter with the dry ingredients until the mixture resembles coarse breadcrumbs. Mix in the egg yolk, then mix in the water one spoon at a time until the dough can be formed into a ball.

Remove, wrap in waxed paper and chill for 30 minutes to 1 hour.

FILLING

1 Tbsp/15 mL olive oil
½ onion, finely chopped
1 tsp/5 mL chili powder
½ tsp/2.5 mL oregano

½ lb/250 g ground beef
¼ cup/50 mL raisins
½ tsp/2.5 mL cayenne pepper
Salt & pepper

Preheat oven to 375°F/190°C.

Heat the oil in a medium frypan over high heat and sauté the meat until browned. Spoon out any excess fat and add the onions. Stir well, add the rest of the ingredients and cook for a further 5 minutes.

Roll out the dough on a floured board and cut into 8 rounds using a saucer or anything round that's handy.

Place 1 Tbsp/15 mL of the filling into the middle of each round. Dampen the edges of the dough with a beaten egg and fold over the meat into half-moon shapes. Prick the pastry with a fork and brush the tops with more of the beaten egg. Bake for 20 minutes.

MAKES 8 EMPANADAS.

Cornish Pasties

To warm the cockles of your heart.

PASTRY

Use the same dough as for Empanadas or 1 packet (8 oz/250 g) frozen shortcrust pastry.

FILLING

1 onion, finely chopped
1 turnip, peeled & grated
Salt & pepper
1 beaten egg

1 potato, peeled & grated
½ lb/250 g ground beef
1 tsp/5 mL butter

Preheat oven to 400°F/200°C.

Roll out the pastry on a floured board and cut out rounds using a saucer. Mix the onion, potato, turnip, beef, salt and pepper together and pile into the middle of each pastry round. Dot each one with butter, dampen the edges with beaten egg, fold over and seal. Cut vents in the pasties, brush with more of the beaten egg and place on a baking tray. Bake for 30 minutes.

MAKES 4 CORNISH PASTIES.

Samosas

Spicy Indian street food. Samosas are to the Indians what Cornish Pasties are to the English.

PASTRY

Use the same dough as for Empanadas or 1 packet (8 oz/250 g) frozen puff pastry.

FILLING

½ onion, chopped
1 potato, cooked & chopped
1 Tbsp/15 mL mustard seeds
½ tsp/2.5 mL curry powder
2 Tbsp/30 mL chopped fresh cilantro

⅓ cup/80 mL cooked peas
1 carrot, cooked & chopped
1 Tbsp/15 mL grated fresh ginger
½ tsp/2.5 mL cayenne pepper

Preheat oven to 375°F/190°C or heat 3 to 4 Tbsp/45 to 60 mL vegetable oil in a large frypan.

Mix all the filling ingredients together. Roll out dough on a floured board and cut into small squares. Place a little of the filling on each square and fold over, sealing the edges, to make small triangles. Fry in the hot oil for about 5 minutes or until brown, or bake for 10 to 15 minutes. Serve with Mango Chutney (page 157).

MAKES 12 SAMOSAS.

Numbkeen

Bits and bites Indian style.

INGREDIENTS

Vegetable oil

Handful of Rice Krispies

Handful of spaghetti & pasta bits

1 tsp/5 mL chili powder

½ tsp/2.5 mL salt

Handful of Corn Flakes

Handful of peanuts

1 tsp/5 mL turmeric

½ tsp/2.5 mL garam masala*

½ tsp/2.5 mL sugar

Heat enough oil to come no more than one-third of the way up a deep saucepan. Fry the Corn Flakes, Rice Krispies, peanuts and pasta bits separately in the oil (that is, fry the Corn Flakes first, take out quickly before they burn, then fry the Rice Krispies, and so on). Drain on paper towels and toss in a bowl with the turmeric, chili powder, garam masala, salt and sugar.

*Available at Indian markets

Chicken & Lettuce Papillote
with Tofu Dressing

(**pap**-ee-yot)

INGREDIENTS

1 tomato, chopped

1 cup/250 mL cooked,
    chopped chicken (skin removed)

Juice of ½ lemon

4 green onions, trimmed

1 hot chili pepper, finely chopped

¼ cup/50 mL chopped olives

2 Tbsp/30 mL chopped fresh cilantro

4 romaine lettuce leaves, blanched

Mix the tomato, chili, chicken, olives, cilantro and lemon juice together and spread over each lettuce leaf. Lay a green onion over the top and wrap the lettuce leaf around the filling. Cover each papillote with cling film and chill for about 1 hour. Serve with Tofu Dressing.

TOFU DRESSING

1 block firm tofu

½ tsp/2.5 mL salt

¼ cup/50 mL vinegar or lemon juice

1 tsp/5 mL maple syrup

¼ cup/50 mL oil

1 clove garlic

Blend all the above ingredients together in a blender or food processor until smooth, adding a little water if necessary.

MAKES 4 CHICKEN AND LETTUCE PAPILLOTES.

Oriental Salad Rolls

Great for summer picnics or take to the office for a quick, healthy lunch.

INGREDIENTS

⅓ packet rice vermicelli*
2 lettuce leaves
2 green onions

2 circles of rice paper*
½ cup/125 mL cooked shrimp

Put the vermicelli noodles into a bowl and pour boiling water over the top. Allow to stand for 5 minutes to soften, then drain.

Dip a piece of rice paper in a bowl of warm water for a few seconds to soften, then remove. Place on a board, fold over one third and lay a lettuce leaf on top. Pile on some noodles and shrimp and lay a green onion over the top (so that it sticks out). Make a tight roll, tucking the ends in, and serve with Peanut Sauce.

PEANUT SAUCE

3 Tbsp/45 mL peanut butter

3 Tbsp/45 mL hoisin sauce*

Heat the peanut butter and hoisin sauce together in a small saucepan over medium heat until almost boiling. Remove and serve. If you don't have hoisin sauce, use apple juice, ½ tsp/2.5 mL cayenne pepper, 1 tsp/5 mL vinegar and 1 Tbsp/15 mL soy sauce.

*Available at Oriental markets
and some supermarkets.

MAKES 2 ORIENTAL SALAD ROLLS.

Oysters & Whiskey

Sinful and delicious.

INGREDIENTS

1 Tbsp/15 mL butter
Salt & pepper
Juice of ½ lemon
6–8 raw oysters, shucked

⅔ cup/160 mL breadcrumbs
2 Tbsp/30 mL olive oil
1 Tbsp/15 mL whiskey

Melt the butter in a frypan over medium heat and gently brown the breadcrumbs. Season with salt and pepper.

In a small bowl, mix together the olive oil, lemon juice and whiskey and drizzle over the oysters. Spoon the fried breadcrumbs on top of each oyster and serve them on cracked ice with lemon wedges to garnish.

SERVES 2 (or just one depending on how much you like oysters).

Onion Cream Tart

Belly-warming winter fare.

PASTRY

2 cups/500 mL flour

1 cup/250 mL butter

Pinch salt

4 Tbsp/60 mL ice-cold water

Preheat the oven to 350°F/180°C.

Sift the flour and salt into a food processor. Cube the butter and add to the flour. Pulse until the mixture resembles coarse breadcrumbs. Add the water one spoon at a time until the dough comes away in a ball.

If making by hand, sift the flour and salt into a large bowl. Cube the butter and work quickly into the flour with your fingertips or a pastry cutter until the mixture resembles coarse breadcrumbs. Add the water slowly until you can form the dough into a ball.

Remove, wrap in waxed paper and chill for 30 minutes to 1 hour.

Press dough into a 9-in/23-cm pie plate. Prick the bottom, cover with foil and bake for 5 to 8 minutes.

FILLING

1 Tbsp/15 mL butter

2 cloves garlic, finely chopped

2 eggs

½ tsp/2.5 mL ground nutmeg

1 onion, sliced into rings

Salt & pepper

½ cup/125 mL light cream

Preheat oven to 350°F/180°C.

Melt the butter in a frypan and sauté the onion rings, garlic, salt and pepper until the onions are soft and translucent. Spoon into the cooked tart shell. Beat the eggs, cream and nutmeg together and pour over the onions.

Bake for 15 minutes. Delicious hot, warm or cold.

SERVES 4.

Crab with Oriental Dipping Sauce

Keep the crab loosely wrapped in an open plastic or paper bag in the fridge or on ice. Don't put it in tap water or it'll die.

INGREDIENTS

1 live crab

Salt

Water

Bring a large saucepan of salted water to the boil. Add the crab, cover and simmer for 15 to 20 minutes. Remove and drain. Pull the legs and claws from the body and crack them with a nut-cracker. Remove the meat and serve crab with Oriental Dipping Sauce.

ORIENTAL DIPPING SAUCE

2 Tbsp/30 mL sherry

1 tsp/5 mL sugar

Juice of ½ lemon

2 Tbsp/30 mL soy sauce

Few drops of tabasco

Mix all the above ingredients together and serve with the cooled crab. This sauce is good for any dipping, or on cold meat.

SERVES 2 (or one as a main course).

Asparagus Pie

So simple and tasty. This makes a great breakfast as well. Throw in some of your favourite herbs for a change.

INGREDIENTS

2 eggs

Salt & pepper

1 small bunch asparagus,
   woody ends removed

½ cup/125 mL cream

4 slices bread

1 cup/250 mL grated cheese (whatever
   you've got that melts well)

Preheat oven to 400°F/200°C.

Beat the eggs, cream, salt and pepper together in a bowl. Dip the bread slices in this mixture and line a small baking dish with them. Arrange the asparagus over the top, sprinkle with cheese and cover with the rest of the egg and cream mixture.

Bake for 20 minutes. Eat hot or cold.

SERVES 2 TO 4.

Easy Pork Pâté

Eat cold as a first course for a smart dinner party, hot on toast with salad for a simple supper dish, on crackers to serve with cocktails, or even cold in sandwiches. The choice is yours!

INGREDIENTS

1 Tbsp/15 mL olive oil

1 onion, chopped

½ tsp/2.5 mL salt

½ tsp/2.5 mL sage

½ tsp/2.5 mL ground cloves

½ cup/125 mL water

1 lb/500 g ground pork

1 garlic clove, chopped

1 tsp/5 mL pepper

1 Tbsp/15 mL mustard

½ tsp/2.5 mL thyme

Heat the oil in a large frypan over high heat and brown the meat. Add the onions and brown. Stir in the rest of the ingredients and cook for 5 to 10 minutes. Remove from the heat and blend in a food processor or blender until it becomes a thick purée.

Serve hot or cold with toast.

SERVES 4.

Spinach & Red Pepper Pizza

Not only delicious but a beautiful work of art! *(See illustration facing page 32.)*

CRUST

5 sheets filo pastry*

4 Tbsp/60 mL Parmesan cheese

2 Tbsp/30 mL melted butter

Preheat oven to 400°F/200°C.

Brush a baking sheet with melted butter, place 1 sheet of filo on top and brush with more butter. Sprinkle with Parmesan cheese and repeat with each layer. Bake for 5 minutes and remove from oven.

TOPPING

2 Tbsp/30 mL olive oil

1 packet frozen spinach

Salt & pepper

2 red peppers, thinly sliced
      into rounds

½ onion, finely chopped

1 clove garlic, finely chopped

½ cup/125 mL feta cheese

Heat 1 Tbsp/15 mL olive oil and sauté the onion until softened. Stir in the spinach and garlic and season with salt and pepper. Spread the spinach onto the filo crust, leaving a border. Sprinkle with the feta cheese and remaining olive oil and scatter with the red pepper. Bake for 15 minutes at the same temperature.

*Available in the frozen-foods section of most supermarkets and some Greek bakeries.

SERVES 4.

Potato Pizza

Good honest peasant fare.

CRUST

1 cup/250 mL flour	*1 tsp/5 mL baking soda*
1 tsp/5 mL cream of tartar	*1 tsp/5 mL salt*
¾ cup/175 mL milk soured	*Olive oil*
* with 1 Tbsp/15 mL vinegar*	

Preheat oven to 475°F/240°C.

For the crust, sift the flour, baking soda, cream of tartar and salt into a bowl. Add the soured milk and stir to make a soft dough. Knead lightly on a floured board to make a ball.

Halve the ball and roll into 2 circles. Place both on a dry, flour-dusted baking sheet. Ridge the edges and brush with olive oil.

TOPPING

1 lb/500 g potatoes	*4 cloves garlic, finely chopped*
Olive oil	*Salt & pepper*
1 Tbsp/15 mL fresh rosemary	*2 Tbsp/30 mL Parmesan cheese*

For the topping, slice the potatoes wafer thin and arrange them in overlapping circles over the dough (like a French apple tart). When the dough is completely covered, scatter the garlic over the 2 pizzas, brush with olive oil and sprinkle with salt, pepper, rosemary and Parmesan. Bake for 20 minutes.

SERVES 4.

Smelts & Wasabi Mayonnaise

(wah-**sah**-bee)

These really aren't as adventurous as they may sound. Smelts are great picnic fare—layer them between sheets of parchment and eat them cold.

INGREDIENTS

1 cup/250 mL breadcrumbs

Salt & pepper

8 fresh smelts

1½ tsp/7.5 mL wasabi* (Japanese
   horseradish) or use
   ordinary horseradish

2 cloves garlic, finely chopped

1 Tbsp/15 mL butter

3 Tbsp/45 mL mayonnaise

Mix together the breadcrumbs, garlic, salt and pepper. Melt the butter, dredge the smelts in the breadcrumb mixture and fry the fish until golden brown on both sides.

Remove and eat either hot or cold with wasabi mayonnaise. Just mix the mayonnaise and wasabi together and serve in a small bowl.

*Available at Japanese markets.

SERVES 4.

Veggie Nachos

A really filling and tasty snack.

INGREDIENTS

1 large packet tortilla chips

1 can corn (10 oz/284 mL) or
   kernels from 1 fresh cob of corn

2 green onions, chopped

½ cup 125 mL tomato salsa

1 cup/250 mL grated cheese (cheddar,
   monterey jack or mozzarella)

1 can black beans (14 oz/398 mL), drained

1 cup/250 mL chopped cilantro

2 tomatoes, chopped

1 can jalapeño peppers (3½ oz/114 mL),
   drained & chopped

Preheat oven to 440°F/200°C.

Arrange tortilla chips on a large baking dish or ovenproof plate. Mix the beans, corn, cilantro, tomatoes, onions, peppers and salsa and spoon over the top. Sprinkle with cheese and bake for 10 to 15 minutes.

Scatter more chopped green onions over the top and serve with sour cream, guacamole and salsa as dips.

Spiced Pecans

Great with cocktails.

INGREDIENTS

1 Tbsp/15 mL olive oil	*2 cups/500 mL pecans*
1 tsp/5 mL chili powder	*1 Tbsp/15 mL soy sauce*
1 tsp/5 mL sugar	*Salt & pepper*

Heat the oil in a large frypan and add the pecans. Stir in the rest of the ingredients and remove when the pecans are well coloured and aromatic, about 5 minutes.

These keep in the freezer forever.

YIELDS 2 CUPS/500 ML.

Broad Bean Purée

No one will guess this tasty dip is just a can of beans!

INGREDIENTS

1 can broad beans (14 oz/398 mL),	*1 onion, sliced*
drained or 1 cup/250 mL	*¼ cup/50 mL olive oil*
cooked fresh broad beans	*½ tsp/2.5 mL cayenne pepper*
Salt & pepper	

Blend all the above ingredients in a food processor or blender until it becomes a thick purée. Tip out into a bowl and sprinkle with a little more olive oil and cayenne pepper. Serve with toast or with taco chips.

Mushroom Tapenade   (**tap-en**-ahd)

A not-so-salty version of the classic.

INGREDIENTS

2 Tbsp/30 mL olive oil	*1 can (3 oz/85 mL) anchovies, drained*
½ lb/250 g mushrooms, finely chopped	*½ cup/125 mL black olives, chopped*
1 clove garlic, chopped	*1 Tbsp/15 mL pistachio nuts, chopped*
2 Tbsp/30 mL parsley, chopped	*Salt & pepper*
Juice of ½ lemon	

Heat the oil in a frypan and stir in the anchovies until they melt. Add the mushrooms, olives, garlic, nuts and parsley. Stir well and add salt, pepper and lemon juice and cook for 5 minutes.

Pour into a bowl and serve hot or cold with fresh vegetables or fried bread or bruschetta (toasted bread).

YIELDS 1 CUP/250 ML.

Salmon, Cream Cheese & Strawberries

Simple and summery.

INGREDIENTS

1 can salmon (7½ oz/213 mL)   ½ cup/125 mL cream cheese
1 Tbsp/15 mL mayonnaise   ½ tsp/2.5 mL dill
Fresh strawberries

Mix the salmon, cream cheese, mayonnaise and dill together in either a food processor or in a bowl using a fork. Mould onto a plate and decorate with sliced strawberries and a fresh dill sprig. Serve with crackers.

Pan Bagna   (pan **ban**-ya)

The ultimate Tuscan Hero.

INGREDIENTS

½ French baguette   1 clove garlic
3 Tbsp/45 mL olive oil   1 tsp/5 mL vinegar
1 can (3 oz/85 mL) anchovies   2–3 tomatoes
2 hard-boiled eggs   ½ cup/125 mL pitted black olives, halved
3 Tbsp/45 mL capers   Pepper

Halve the stick lengthwise, open out and rub each half with the garlic. Sprinkle with olive oil and vinegar. Drain the anchovies and arrange over one half. Slice the tomatoes and eggs and lay on top. Scatter the olives and capers on top, sprinkle with pepper and sandwich together.

Wrap tightly in cling film or foil, place a weight on top and leave to stand at room temperature for 1 to 2 hours. Serve in thick slices.

SERVES 2.

Stuffed Pita Bread

This really is good. Trust me.

INGREDIENTS

1 Tbsp/15 mL butter

1 tsp/5 mL pepper

2 pita breads

Salt

Mango chutney

2 cups/500 mL cooked, mashed potato

1 Tbsp/15 mL curry powder

2 Tbsp/30 mL chopped cilantro or parsley

1–2 Tbsp/30 mL yoghurt

½ small cucumber

Melt the butter in a frypan and fry the potatoes, pepper and curry powder. Add the cilantro and toss well together. Halve and open out each pita bread and stuff with the potato mixture. Season with a little salt and top with yoghurt.

Serve with Mango Chutney (page 157) and sliced cucumber.

SERVES 2.

Anchovy Pâté Sandwiches

Anchovies . . . ! I know but just *try* it!

INGREDIENTS

8 oz/250 g cream cheese

1 tsp/5 mL freshly ground black pepper

Shredded lettuce

1 can (3 oz/85 mL) anchovies, drained

12 slices of bread

Blend the cream cheese, anchovies and pepper in a food processor or hand mixer and spread over 6 of the slices of bread. Top with shredded lettuce or sprouts and sandwich together with the other 6 bread slices.

MAKES 6 SANDWICHES.

Fried Ravioli with Tomato & Basil Salsa

A nice surprise to serve with cocktails.

INGREDIENTS

½ lb/250 g fresh ravioli (uncooked)

1 egg, beaten with 1 Tbsp/15 mL milk

½ cup/125 mL breadcrumbs mixed
   with ½ cup/125 mL Parmesan cheese

2 Tbsp/30 mL flour

4 Tbsp/60 mL olive oil

Dredge the ravioli in flour, then in the egg and milk mixture and coat with breadcrumbs and cheese. Heat the oil in a large frypan and sauté the ravioli until golden brown. Serve on toothpicks with Tomato and Basil Salsa.

TOMATO AND BASIL SALSA

3 tomatoes, chopped

1 clove garlic, minced

1 bunch fresh basil, chopped

Salt & pepper

Mix all the above ingredients together and serve with fried ravioli.

SERVES 6.

Zucchini & Tomato Spread

One of the few dips that are relatively low in fat.

INGREDIENTS

2 Tbsp/30 mL olive oil

6 whole cloves garlic

½ lb/250 g zucchini, chopped

½ tsp/2.5 mL chili powder

Salt & pepper

1 onion, chopped

1 tsp/5 mL ground cumin

1 Tbsp/15 mL vinegar

½ lb/250 g tomatoes, chopped

Heat the oil in a large frypan over high heat and sauté the onion until browned. Stir in the rest of the ingredients, cover and cook for 8 to 10 minutes. Mash the mixture with a potato masher or blend in the food processor and serve cold with toasts.

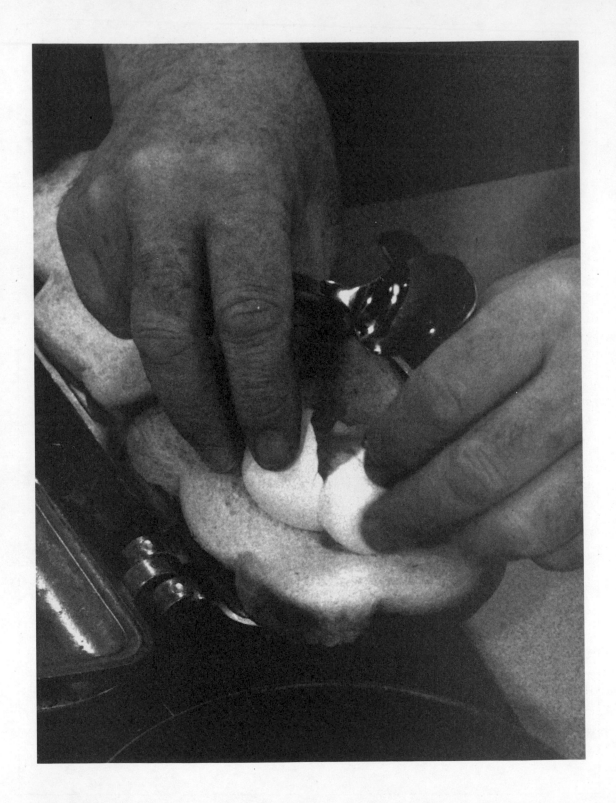

Soups

Soup is good any time of year. But when winter arrives it's Soup Time— none of your fancy consommés, or delicate little fruit soups, but time for some real gutsy solid soup—what the French call knife and fork soups and the Germans call belly warmers. The first thing you need to know about soup (in fact just about the only thing) is that good soups don't come out of a can, or a package, or a microwave. Soup is cooking with your heart, it's a state of mind, soup is something that spreads a nice warm glow over the whole house,

it's not something just to eat, it's something to wait for and anticipate, it's a present to yourself and everybody else that eats it, it's a statement of love and caring and if you think that sounds all sloppy and kissy like a Harlequin romance, then you're wrong, it's not that at all, it's the same kind of care as artists talk about, it's time and energy put into making the best you can out of just what you've got, and then being very proud of the end result. ■ But soup is not as difficult as painting. Anybody who is basically kind can make good soup. You

don't have to be a kitchen wizard or a graduate of a fancy French cooking school, and you don't need fancy pots, any old saucepan will do, and it's easy. EASY EASY EASY, and here's how you do it, the basic, world-wide recipe for soup, or soup you can make out of just about everything. ■ If you're the kind of person who has to write things down then grab a pencil right now. Got it? And some paper? Now, one onion, a big one. You can't make an omelette without breaking eggs and you can't make soup without an onion. Chop it up small, melt 2 Tbsp of butter over medium heat, and cook the onion for 3 minutes, stirring it around. Add a good big teaspoon of ground pepper, and a big potato, or two medium ones, cut into dice a bit smaller than sugar cubes. Stir everything around to coat it with butter and onion juice, then add four cups of liquid. What kind of liquid? Water. That's right, water, no fancy stocks, no expensive wines, just water. Bring it to the boil, and simmer for 20 minutes, until the potato is soft. Mash it with a big fork or a potato masher, but leave a few lumps, stir in about a teaspoon of salt, and, if you've got it, a pinch of nutmeg. That's it, a potato soup, a potage as the gourmets would say, a great soup for right now, or for lunch if your office has a microwave. You can add almost anything to this basic recipe. A grated carrot and a chopped tomato with a little oregano will make it Italiana, a sort of minestrone, or if you run it through the food processor and add a little cream it will be French. If you add some chunks of salami it's sort of Polish—that's all you really need to know—and just remember not to fuss too much. I'd rather be loved for my soup than my bald head. ■

Garlic Soup & Poached Eggs

My grandfather used to say that a clove of raw garlic every day keeps colds away.

INGREDIENTS

1 Tbsp/15 mL butter

½ onion, chopped

Salt & pepper

2 eggs

5 cloves garlic, chopped

2 cups/500 mL chicken stock

2 slices bread, torn up

Chopped parsley

Melt the butter and sauté the garlic and onion in a saucepan over medium heat until softened. Add the stock and bring to a boil. Season with black pepper and a little salt and stir in the bread. Turn down the heat and simmer for a further 5 minutes.

Break each egg onto a saucer and gently slide into the soup. Serve when the eggs are gently poached and sprinkle with chopped parsley.

SERVES 2.

Potage St. Germain

(**paw**-tazh)

Good soothing green pea soup.

INGREDIENTS

2 Tbsp/30 mL butter

1 onion, chopped

Chopped parsley

1 packet frozen green peas
   (or fresh, or canned)

Light cream to taste

1 small head lettuce, chopped

2 stalks celery, chopped

2 cups/500 mL chicken stock

Salt & Pepper

Mint

Sherry to taste

Melt the butter and sauté the lettuce, onion, celery and parsley in a saucepan over medium heat. Add the chicken stock and peas and simmer until soft. Season with salt, pepper and mint.

Blend and serve either hot or cold with a swirl of light cream, sherry and fresh mint.

SERVES 2.

Cream of Mushroom Soup

Nothing like the store-bought version. This is worth that little extra effort.

INGREDIENTS

2 Tbsp/30 mL butter

1 clove garlic, chopped

Salt & pepper

2 cups/500 mL chicken stock

½ tsp/2.5 mL nutmeg

½ cup/125 mL whipping
   cream or yoghurt

½ onion, chopped

½ lb/250 g mushrooms, sliced

1 Tbsp/15 mL mustard

1 tsp/5 mL dill

2–3 oz/50–75 mL sherry

Garlic croutons

Melt the butter and sauté the onion and garlic in a medium saucepan. Add mushrooms, salt and pepper and stir well. Cover and cook over low heat for 5 minutes. Stir in the mustard, stock, dill and nutmeg, bring to a boil and cook for 5 minutes. Stir in sherry, add cream or yoghurt and blend until smooth.

Serve sprinkled with garlic croutons.

SERVES 2.

Kidney Bean Soup

Be a little more liberal with the spices if you like.

INGREDIENTS

1 Tbsp/15 mL oil or butter

2 cloves garlic, chopped

1 can (14 oz/398 mL) red
   kidney beans, drained & rinsed

Stock (chicken, beef or vegetable)
   or water as required

1 onion, chopped

1 can (13 oz/370 mL) chopped tomatoes

½ tsp/2.5 mL cumin or oregano

1 tsp/5 mL chili powder

Heat the oil in a saucepan and sauté the onions and garlic. Add the beans, tomatoes, and seasonings and enough stock or water to just cover. Simmer 5 to 10 minutes and blend in a food processor or blender.

Serve with chopped chives, sour cream or coriander.

SERVES 2.

Cold Tomato Soup

Nothing is better when the tomatoes are at their peak in the fall. *(See illustration on overleaf facing page 32.)*

INGREDIENTS

2 cups/500 mL ripe tomatoes

Fresh parsley

Juice of ½ orange or lemon

1 cup/250 mL cream

Fresh basil

Salt & pepper

Blend all the above ingredients in a food processor and serve well chilled, garnished with orange or lemon zest and basil leaves.

SERVES 2.

Cold Watermelon & Cucumber Soup

For a great presentation, serve this in a hollowed-out watermelon.

INGREDIENTS

4 cups watermelon chunks

1 cup/250 mL yoghurt

2 cucumbers, peeled & chopped

Blend all the above ingredients in a food processor or blender and serve well chilled.

SERVES 4.

Avocado Cream

Throw a dollop of this in your next soup. Especially good with tomato soup.

INGREDIENTS

2 avocados, mashed

Juice of ½ lemon

1 clove garlic

Salt & pepper

Blend all the above ingredients and add to soups as a garnish or swirled in.

MAKES 1 CUP/250 ML.

Cold Carrot Soup

A cold treat to serve on those hot summer days.

INGREDIENTS

6 carrots	1 cup/250 mL chicken stock
½ cup/125 mL orange juice	1 cup/250 mL whipping cream or yoghurt
¼ tsp/1 mL nutmeg	Salt & pepper
Chopped mint or coriander	

Cook the carrots until tender and drain. Purée with the rest of the ingredients, reserving the mint or coriander for garnish. Chill and serve.

SERVES 4.

Raw Carrot Soup or Drink

Here's to your health!

INGREDIENTS

2 carrots, grated	2 slices fresh ginger
Pinch salt	Pinch pepper
2 cups/500 mL apple juice	Handful fresh parsley
Lemon juice to taste	

Blend all the above ingredients in a blender or food processor until smooth and pour into a bowl or tall glass.

SERVES 1.

Oyster & Artichoke Soup

An exotic opening to an elegant entrée.

INGREDIENTS

2 Tbsp/30 mL butter	Pepper
3 green onions, chopped	½ lb/250 g oysters
1 can artichoke hearts, drained & quartered	1 cup/250 mL whipping cream
	Parsley, chopped
Salt	1 glass white wine (or de-alcoholized wine)

Spinach & Red Pepper Pizza *(see recipe on page 17)*

Cold Tomato Soup *(see recipe on page 31)*

North African Chicken *(see recipe on page 46)*

Chicken in Papaya Skin *(see recipe on page 47)*

Melt the butter in a saucepan, add the pepper and the chopped onion (white part only) and sauté for 2 to 3 minutes. Add the oysters, cook for 2 to 3 minutes and add the artichoke hearts. Pour in the cream, chopped parsley and wine and sprinkle with a pinch of salt. Bring to a boil and serve, garnished with the chopped onion greens.

SERVES 2.

Cold Mango & Carrot Soup

Serve in chilled soup bowls.

INGREDIENTS

1 Tbsp/15 mL oil
1 onion, chopped
1 potato, grated
1 tsp/5 mL cumin seeds
1 tsp/5 mL coriander seeds
½ tsp/2.5 mL pepper
1 mango, chopped
Yoghurt

1 Tbsp/15 mL butter
1 celery stick, chopped
2 carrots, grated
1 tsp/5 mL cardamom seeds
½ tsp/2.5 mL salt
1 cup/250 mL chicken stock and/or apple juice
Cilantro or parsley, chopped

Heat the oil and butter in a saucepan and sauté the onion. Stir in the celery, potato and carrots and lightly brown. Add the cumin, cardamom, coriander, salt and pepper and pour in the stock. Cook until the vegetables are softened.

Pour into a food processor or blender, add the mango and process until smooth and creamy. Chill. Serve with chopped cilantro or parsley and yoghurt.

SERVES 2.

French Onion Soup

Everyone's favourite.

INGREDIENTS

2 Tbsp/30 mL butter
2 cups/500 mL beef stock
1 tsp/5 mL tarragon
1 Tbsp/15 mL chopped mushrooms
2 slices French bread

2 onions, thinly sliced
1 glass red or white wine or apple juice
½ tsp/2.5 mL black pepper
Dash of brandy
½ cup/125 mL grated cheese (Swiss, Gruyère, Jarlsberg or whatever else you have on hand)

Melt the butter in a saucepan and sauté the onions over medium-low heat until well browned and caramelized. Pour in the stock, wine, tarragon and pepper and simmer for 10 minutes. Stir in the mushrooms and brandy and pour into two bowls.

Lay a slice of bread on top of each bowl of soup, cover with grated cheese and put under the broiler for 1 to 2 minutes, until the cheese has melted.

SERVES 2.

Swagman Soup

The "anything goes"/"what you have in the bush" soup.

INGREDIENTS

2 Tbsp/30 mL oil

1 leek, chopped

½ potato, grated

1 stick celery, chopped

1 tsp/5 mL cloves

1 cup/250 mL beef stock

1 onion, chopped

1 turnip, chopped

1 carrot, chopped

1 tsp/5 mL black pepper

½ tsp/2.5 mL salt

1 can beer or water

Heat the oil in a saucepan and sauté the vegetables until browned and softened. Add the pepper, cloves, salt, stock and beer. Simmer for 10 minutes and serve with chopped parsley.

SERVES 2.

Chickpea & Turnip Soup

A belly warmer.

INGREDIENTS

2 Tbsp/30 mL olive oil

1 medium onion, chopped

2 stalks celery

1 cup/250 mL stock

½ head lettuce, shredded

Chopped parsley

2 cloves garlic, chopped

1 medium turnip, chopped

1 28-oz/796-mL can chickpeas, drained

Salt & pepper

Grated cheese

Heat the oil in a saucepan and sauté the garlic, onion, turnip and celery. Add the chickpeas, stock, salt and pepper and simmer for 15 minutes. Stir in the lettuce for the last 5 minutes and serve sprinkled with grated cheese and chopped parsley.

SERVES 4.

Cream of Banana Soup

Another name for Scotch bonnet peppers is Cuban Habañero peppers. Either way, they're THE hottest in the world. Wear gloves when chopping them.

INGREDIENTS

4 bananas, ripe
1 cup/250 mL stock
⅓ cup/80 mL cream
Salt & pepper

1 tsp/5 mL minced Scotch bonnet chili pepper
2 cups/500 mL water
1 Tbsp/15 mL rum
Red & yellow peppers

Peel and chop the bananas. Purée with the chili in a food processor or blender and pour into a saucepan. Heat gently and add the stock and water. Cook for 5 minutes. Add cream, rum, salt and pepper to taste, and bring to the boil. Serve hot with julienned red and yellow peppers or cilantro as garnish.

SERVES 4.

Red Pepper Soup in Bread Bowls

Take the time to have a little fun with your presentations. Food should be pleasing to the eye as well as the palate.

INGREDIENTS

2 small rounds of bread
   (sourdough or French)
1 Tbsp/15 mL breadcrumbs
2 tomatoes, chopped
1 Tbsp/15 mL tomato paste
Salt & pepper

2 Tbsp/30 mL oil
1 onion, chopped
2 red peppers, chopped
1 clove garlic, chopped
1 tsp/5 mL thyme
2 cups/500 mL chicken stock or apple juice

Preheat oven to 350°F/180°C.

Hollow out bread loaves, brush with oil and bake for 10 minutes. Heat 2 Tbsp/30 mL oil in a frypan and sauté the onion, breadcrumbs and peppers until softened. Add the tomatoes, garlic, tomato paste and thyme and pour in the stock or apple juice. Season with salt and pepper and allow to simmer for 5 to 10 minutes.

Pour into the baked loaves and serve in bowls. For a smoother consistency, you can blend the soup in a food processor or blender just before serving.

SERVES 2.

Strawberry, Watermelon, Cucumber & Wine Soup

Soup fit for a very special occasion. Appetizer or dessert.

INGREDIENTS

3 cups strawberries

1 cup/250 mL cucumber chunks

½ cup/125 mL orange juice

1 Tbsp/15 mL black pepper

½ cup/125 mL yoghurt

3 cups watermelon chunks

½ bottle wine or de-alcoholized wine

1 Tbsp/15 mL honey

1 tsp/5 mL vanilla

Blend all the ingredients in a blender or food processor, pour into bowls and chill. Decorate with sliced cucumbers, tiny shrimp and fresh mint leaves.

SERVES 4.

Chicken Consommé in Silver Teapot (or any old teapot)

Perfect for leftover chicken—and how elegant!

INGREDIENTS

1 Tbsp/15 mL oil

1 cooked chicken breast, minced

3 Tbsp/45 mL sherry

Salt & pepper

Juice of 1 lemon

1 onion, minced

1 Tbsp/15 mL soy sauce

Zest of ½ orange

2–3 prawns, peeled & minced

Heat the oil and soften the onion until transparent, not brown. Stir in the chicken and add the soy sauce, sherry, orange zest, salt and pepper. Add 1 cup/250 mL of water and bring to the boil. Add the prawns and lemon juice and pour into a teapot.

Allow to steep for 1 to 2 minutes. Take the teapot to the table and pour into bowls. Decorate with flowers.

SERVES 2.

Poultry

hicken is one of the few things that the average cook, surrounded by the symphony of disasters that makes up a family kitchen, can bring to the table looking as good as, if not better than, the pictures in the glossy food magazines. ■ Almost any chicken dish looks good. Baked, boiled, fried, steamed, poached, stewed or barbecued, there's very little you can do to a chicken to make it look like anything but a nice piece of chicken. You can cook it with breadcrumbs, with nuts, fruit, even peanut butter or marmalade and it still finishes up glamorous. ■ Most kids like chicken, even those who think that a can of spaghetti is the food of the gods, and the only religion chicken offends is vegetarian. It pleases almost everybody—there's white meat, dark meat, some pieces with a bone and some without. Dragged out of a dark corner of the freezer one Saturday night when company comes uninvited and looks as if it won't leave before supper, almost any old bit of chicken lends itself to immediate improvisation—a few beans, a can of tomatoes, maybe some pasta—there's supper, and if you're

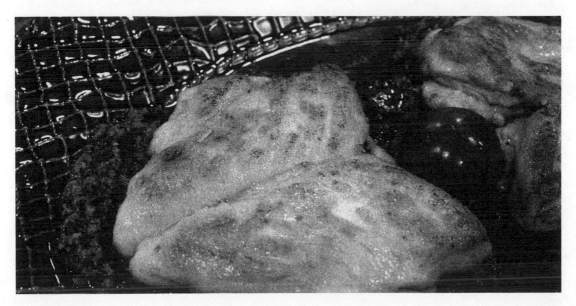

bright enough to give it a fancy name ("Pollo Venezio"—my great-great-grandma was Italian . . .) people will invariably like it, and ask you for the recipe. ■ But despite this versatility, chicken still brings out the conservative in our kitchens. The recent U.S. study which showed that most families had a maximum repertoire of 10 recipes (including such things as packaged hotcakes, lasagne and muffin mix) also showed that chicken, *fried,* was one invariable constant. There's nothing wrong with that—dinner in a hurry, cooked on top of the stove—but there are alternatives to Shake 'n Bake. Flip channels occasionally—try something different—you don't watch the same movie every night, so give your tastebuds a holiday. ■ You can pretty it up with chopped parsley, or chopped spring onion tops, or chopped chives. You can eat it with asparagus or a salad; you can add a handful of black pepper if you want it Szechuan style and spicy; you can sprinkle it with lemon juice; you can add a glass of sherry to the pan for the last two minutes of cooking—there's almost nothing in the fridge that won't improve your basic chicken recipe. You don't need me or any fancy cook to tell you how to be inventive with chicken—just pretend you're a kid all over again, with finger paints, and see what happens. A few slices of fresh ginger, 20 garlic cloves (yeah, 20, don't peel them, just fry them with the chicken) or even just finish up with the plain chicken dusted all over with fine chopped parsley and sprinkled with lemon juice. Try a handful of grapes in the pan, with a little tarragon. Fry some slices of apple along with the chicken, then dust it all with cinnamon. Fry chunks of banana with it, sprinkled with curry powder. Go on, try it now, open the fridge, take out the chicken and whatever else you fancy, and I guarantee it won't disappoint you. And while turkey and duck and quail and the whole line-up of poultry may not be quite as versatile as chicken, they too benefit from many kitchen inventions. ■

The Best Fried Chicken in the World: Chicken & Peach Sauce

INGREDIENTS

Vegetable oil
½ cup/125 mL milk
1 cup/250 mL flour
¼ cup/50 mL yellow cornmeal
½ tsp/2.5 mL paprika

1 egg
½ tsp/2.5 mL black pepper
½ tsp/2.5 mL salt
½ tsp/2.5 mL baking powder
4 chicken thighs

Heat enough vegetable oil to come no more than one-third of the way up a medium-sized saucepan. (Keep a lid handy to put on top of the saucepan just in case of fire.)

Meanwhile, beat the egg, milk and pepper in one bowl. In another bowl mix the rest of the dry ingredients.

Test to see if the oil is hot enough by dropping small pieces of bread in. When it sizzles immediately when you drop it in and starts to brown, the oil is hot enough.

Dip the chicken first in the egg mixture, then in the flour mixture and fry until golden brown and crispy, about 8 to 10 minutes. Serve with Peach Sauce.

PEACH SAUCE

½ can (14 oz/398 mL) sliced
  peaches & juice
Juice of a lemon
½ cup/125 mL water
3 Tbsp/45 mL brown sugar
1 Tbsp/15 mL butter
1 Tbsp/15 mL vinegar
½ tsp/2.5 mL paprika
Pinch salt
Pinch cayenne pepper

Stir all the above ingredients in a medium saucepan over low heat until it's turned itself into a thick and syrupy sauce, about 10 minutes.

SERVES 2.

Apricot Chicken

Gourmet taste without the hassle.

INGREDIENTS

1/3 cup/80 mL apricot jam

1 tsp/5 mL Dijon mustard

*1 whole boneless chicken
     breast, halved & skinned*

1 Tbsp/15 mL soy sauce

1 tsp/5 mL honey

1 tsp/5 mL butter

Mix all the ingredients together, except the chicken, in a bowl. Place the chicken on a baking sheet and brush with the apricot mixture. Broil for 5 minutes each side, basting with more mixture if necessary.

SERVES 2.

Chicken & Rhubarb

The rhubarb gives a sweet and sour tanginess to this dish.

INGREDIENTS

*1 whole boneless chicken breast,
     skinned & halved*

2 Tbsp/30 mL vegetable oil

2 sticks rhubarb, finely chopped

1 tsp/5 mL black pepper

1/3 cup/80 mL white wine

3 green onions, chopped

2 Tbsp/30 mL flour

1 Tbsp/15 mL curry powder

1 onion, chopped

1 Tbsp/15 mL brown sugar

1 tsp/5 mL tarragon (or dill)

2 Tbsp/30 mL chopped fresh parsley

Shake the chicken, flour and curry powder together in a plastic bag and remove the lightly dusted chicken.

Heat the oil in a large, deep-sided frypan over high heat and add the onions and rhubarb. Cook until softened and lightly browned, turn down the heat and stir in the brown sugar, pepper and tarragon.

Push the mixture to the sides of the pan and lay the chicken breasts in the middle. Brown the chicken (about 5 minutes each side), pour in the wine, and reduce for 2 to 3 minutes.

Add the chopped parsley and green onions, stir well and serve immediately with rice.

SERVES 2.

Chicken Papillote

This quick way of cooking seals in all the juices of the chicken, keeping it very tender.

INGREDIENTS

1 whole boneless chicken breast,
   skinned, halved and pounded thin
2 carrots, julienned
Juice of a lemon or orange
2 Tbsp/30 mL brandy

1 Tbsp/15 mL olive oil
2 leeks, julienned
Handful of grapes (preferably seedless)
1 Tbsp/15 mL fresh thyme
Salt & pepper

Preheat oven to 400°F/200°C.

Cut out two very large heart shapes or squares from a piece of foil and drizzle oil over the shiny side. Place a chicken breast on one half of each piece of foil and scatter the vegetables and grapes over it.

Sprinkle with lemon juice, thyme, brandy, salt and pepper, fold the foil over and seal the two packages. Bake for 10 to 12 minutes.

SERVES 2.

Chicken & Lychees

(**lee**-chee)

Lychees have a wonderful perfume and can sometimes be found fresh wrapped in their brittle shells in supermarkets or Oriental markets. But if you can't find them—either fresh or in the can—substitute grapes or canned cherries or any other fruit that will add just a touch of sweetness to the dish.

INGREDIENTS

2 Tbsp/30 mL vegetable oil
3 green onions, chopped
2 cloves garlic, chopped
1 can (14 oz/398 mL) lychees, drained*
1 Tbsp/15 mL sesame oil

1 whole boneless chicken breast, skinned & cubed
3 slices fresh ginger, finely chopped
2 Tbsp/30 mL soy sauce
½ cup/125 mL shredded lettuce
Cooked noodles (whatever type you like)

Heat the oil in a large deep-sided frypan over high heat and sauté the chicken cubes and green onions until lightly browned. Stir in the ginger, garlic and soy sauce, cook for 1 minute and stir in the lychees and shredded lettuce. Cook for another half a minute and stir in the sesame oil.

Serve immediately over hot noodles.

*Available at Oriental markets and most supermarkets.

SERVES 2.

Rhubarb Fool & Chicken

INGREDIENTS

1 whole boneless chicken
   breast, skinned & halved
2 Tbsp/30 mL vegetable oil
Mint leaves

2 Tbsp/30 mL flour
1 Tbsp/15 mL curry powder
Rhubarb Fool (see below)
Freshly ground black pepper

Shake the chicken, flour and curry powder in a plastic bag and remove the lightly dusted chicken.

Heat the oil in a medium-sized frypan over high heat and sauté the breasts until browned on both sides (about 5 minutes each side) and the inside flesh is cooked but still moist.

Make a pool of Rhubarb Fool on a plate and lay the chicken breasts on top. Decorate with mint leaves and sprinkle with freshly ground black pepper.

SERVES 2.

COLD RHUBARB FOOL

1 Tbsp/15 mL butter
3 slices fresh ginger, grated
¾ cup/175 mL yoghurt

3 Tbsp/45 mL brown sugar
2 cups/500 mL coarsely chopped rhubarb
Mint leaves

Melt the butter in a medium saucepan over medium heat and stir in the brown sugar and ginger. Add the rhubarb, stir well to coat each piece with butter and sugar, turn the heat down and cover. Simmer until soft, about 5 to 10 minutes.

Remove from the heat and let cool. Blend in a food processor or blender and fold in the yoghurt.

Serve as Rhubarb Fool and Chicken above or pour into glass dishes and decorate with mint leaves for dessert.

MAKES ABOUT 2 CUPS/500 ML.

> It is important to wash hands, utensils and cutting board immediately after touching raw poultry because nearly half of all raw chicken contains salmonella bacteria (which is destroyed in the cooking process) and the bacteria can be transferred easily.

Thai Red Curry Chicken

Simpler than you think. Try it!

INGREDIENTS

1 whole boneless chicken breast, skinned

3 Tbsp/45 mL white wine

1 can (14 oz/398 mL) coconut milk

2 tsp/10 mL red curry paste* (1 tsp/5 mL for milder)

1 Tbsp/15 mL fish sauce* (naam pla) or 1 anchovy

1 cup/250 mL chopped frozen spinach, thawed (or fresh, cooked)

1 red bell pepper, julienned

Basil leaves

Cut chicken breasts into long, narrow pieces and marinate in white wine for at least 15 minutes. Remove and steam for 5 minutes, turn heat off and allow to sit for 2 to 3 more minutes.

Heat the coconut milk in a medium saucepan (but don't boil) and stir in the curry paste and fish sauce. Add the spinach, red pepper and chicken pieces and heat through for 3 to 4 minutes.

Serve over rice and garnish with basil leaves.

*Available at Asian markets.

SERVES 2.

New Orleans Dirty Rice

This spicy dish is a great way to use up leftover rice. A delicious one-plate meal.

INGREDIENTS

2 Tbsp/30 mL vegetable oil

¾ lb/375 g chicken livers, halved & the membrane removed

Salt & pepper

3 Tbsp/45 mL fresh parsley, chopped

2 Tbsp/30 mL flour

1 onion, chopped

2 red chilis, chopped

2 cups/500 mL cooked rice

2 Tbsp/30 mL nuts, chopped

Heat the oil in a large deep-sided frypan over high heat. Shake the chicken livers and flour in a plastic bag to coat them lightly, remove from the bag and put them into the hot oil. When the livers are lightly browned, stir in the chopped onion and chilis. Brown the onions, season with salt and pepper and stir in the cooked rice.

Cook for about 5 to 8 minutes or until everything is well mixed and heated through and add the chopped parsley and nuts. Tip onto a large platter and serve with more chopped parsley.

SERVES 2.

North African Chicken

Serve this traditional chicken dish with couscous, rice or pita bread and sweet mint leaf tea. *(See illustration on overleaf facing page 33.)*

INGREDIENTS

2 Tbsp/30 mL vegetable oil

½ tsp/2.5 mL cayenne pepper

4 green onions, cut into lengths

1 tsp/5 mL ground coriander

Salt & pepper

Juice of 1 lemon

1 whole boneless chicken breast, skinned & halved

3 cloves garlic, chopped

3 slices ginger, finely chopped

1 cup/250 mL chopped peanuts, toasted

1 cup/250 mL chicken stock or coconut milk

Cut the chicken into strips. Heat the oil in a large frypan over high heat and fry the chicken strips and cayenne pepper. Stir in the garlic, green onions, ginger and peanuts and sprinkle with coriander, salt and pepper.

Pour in the stock or coconut milk and lemon juice, stir well for another minute and serve with more chopped green onions and fresh coriander.

SERVES 2.

Five Spice Powder Chicken

Not always exactly five spices, five spice powder is usually a combination of star anise, cinnamon, cloves, fennel and Sczechuan peppercorns, with the addition sometimes of ground ginger. A very distinct, almost sweet flavour.

INGREDIENTS

1 Tbsp/15 mL cornstarch

1 whole boneless chicken breast,
    skinned & cut into strips

½ green bell pepper, julienned

1 tsp/5 mL sesame oil

1 tsp/5 mL five spice powder

1 Tbsp/15 mL vegetable oil

1 onion, chopped

1 Tbsp/15 mL freshly ground black pepper

Shake the cornstarch, five spice powder and chicken together in a plastic bag and remove the lightly dusted chicken strips. Heat the oil in a medium frypan over high heat and brown the chicken. Add the onion, green pepper and black pepper and stir well for 1 to 2 minutes. Sprinkle with sesame oil and serve.

SERVES 2.

Spatchcocked Quail & Grapes

The word "spatchcocking" comes from 18th-century Ireland where, on the unexpected arrival of guests, a chicken was quickly "dispatched" or killed and then split open and cooked. Basically it means "squashed" quails.

INGREDIENTS

4 quails, spatchcocked

2 egg whites, beaten

1 Tbsp/15 mL butter

2 cloves garlic, chopped

½ cup/125 mL fresh cilantro
  or parsley, chopped

3 Tbsp/45 mL olive oil

4 Tbsp/60 mL fine cornmeal

½ cup/125 mL almonds

½ cup/125 mL grapes (preferably seedless)

Using a pair of sharp scissors, cut through the backbone of each quail without separating the two halves and open them out. Flatten each one and dry well with paper towels.

Heat the oil in a large frypan over high heat. Dip the quails in beaten egg whites and then cornmeal. Fry until they're brown on both sides (about 5 to 6 minutes each side) and remove to a warmed platter.

Turn the heat down to medium-low and add the butter, almonds, garlic and grapes. Sauté for 2 to 3 minutes and stir in the chopped cilantro. Pour over the quails and serve with hot noodles.

SERVES 4.

Chicken in Papaya Skin

The papaya keeps the chicken nice and juicy and tenderizes it too. (See illustration facing page 33.)

INGREDIENTS

1 whole boneless chicken breast,
  skinned & halved

2 chilis, finely chopped
  or 1 tsp/5 mL chili flakes

Juice of 1 lime

½ onion, finely chopped

2 cloves garlic, chopped

½ tsp/2.5 mL salt

2 Tbsp/30 mL chopped fresh cilantro

2 papayas, halved, seeded & slightly scooped out

Preheat oven to 350°F/180°C.

Pound the chicken breasts (with a rolling pin or wine bottle) between floured waxed paper until thin and nearly double their original size.

Mix the onion, garlic, chilis, salt, cilantro and lime juice together in a bowl. Spoon half the mixture onto one end of a chicken breast and carefully roll up. Repeat with the other one.

Place a chicken roll into each papaya half, cover with the other papaya half and bake for 25 minutes.

SERVES 2.

Chicken & Strawberries

Very romantic . . .

INGREDIENTS

1 Tbsp/15 mL butter
1 whole boneless chicken breast,
    skinned, halved & pounded thin
½ tsp/2.5 mL curry powder (optional)
1 glass white wine or apple juice
Pinch salt
Chopped fresh mint

1 Tbsp/15 mL vegetable oil
1 Tbsp/15 mL black pepper
3 green onions, cut into lengths
2 Tbsp/30 mL crystallized ginger, chopped
Juice of 1 small orange
2 cups/500 mL sliced strawberries

Heat the butter and oil in a frypan over medium heat and sauté the chicken breasts and pepper until the chicken is lightly browned on both sides (about 5 minutes each side). Add the green onions, curry powder and chopped ginger and stir for half a minute. Pour in the wine, orange juice and a pinch of salt, stir well and add the strawberries.

Stir gently for 1 minute and tip onto a platter. Decorate with fresh mint leaves.

SERVES 2.

Chicken, Pears & Apples

This one always makes me think of the autumn.

INGREDIENTS

1 whole boneless chicken
    breast, skinned & halved
⅓ cup/80 mL olive oil
Juice of 1 orange
1 tsp/5 mL cayenne pepper
Fresh basil leaves

2 pears, cored & halved
2 apples, cored & halved
2 Tbsp/30 mL cider vinegar
1 tsp/5 mL black pepper
1 Tbsp/15 mL fresh rosemary, chopped

Marinate the chicken, pears and apples in the oil, vinegar, orange juice, pepper, cayenne pepper and rosemary for about 1 hour.

Heat a large frypan (no oil) over high heat and fry the chicken, pears and apples until well browned (about 5 minutes each side). Serve garnished with fresh basil leaves.

SERVES 2.

Mexican Pickled Turkey Breast

A nice twist for this versatile meat.

INGREDIENTS

1 turkey breast, poached
   in wine or stock
4 cloves garlic, finely chopped
1 Tbsp/15 mL oregano
1 Tbsp/15 mL peppercorns
1 cup/250 mL vinegar

2 Tbsp/30 mL olive oil
1 onion, sliced
4 bay leaves, crumbled
1 Tbsp/15 mL allspice
1 Tbsp/15 mL sugar
Salt

Heat all the ingredients except the turkey in a saucepan. Bring to a boil and turn off the heat. Let sit for a while.

Pour over the turkey breast and allow to stand for 1 hour or overnight. Slice and serve in sandwiches.

Turkey Dianne

Good with chicken too.

INGREDIENTS

½ cup/125 mL ground almonds
Salt & pepper
2 Tbsp/30 mL olive oil

2 Tbsp/30 mL Parmesan cheese
2 turkey breast fillets

Preheat the oven to 375°F/190°C.

Mix the ground almonds, Parmesan cheese, salt and pepper together. Brush the turkey breasts with olive oil and cover each one with the almond mixture. Lay on a greased baking sheet and cook for 25 minutes.

SERVES 2.

Turkey Fricassee

Comfort food for a cold, wet day.

INGREDIENTS

½ lb/250 g turkey meat, cubed
Salt & pepper
2 Tbsp/30 mL olive oil
1 glass white wine
2 egg yolks

3–4 Tbsp/45–60 mL flour
1 tsp/5 mL oregano
1 onion, finely chopped
½ cup/125 mL stock
Juice of 2 lemons

Dredge the turkey cubes in flour seasoned with salt, pepper and oregano. Heat the oil in a frypan and sauté the meat until light brown. Add the onions, sprinkle with salt and stir in the wine and stock.

Keep the heat up fairly high and cook until most of the liquid has evaporated and the turkey is tender. (Add more liquid if the turkey takes longer to cook.) Turn off the heat.

Beat the egg yolks and *slowly* squeeze in the lemon juice while continuing to beat so that you have an emulsion. Quickly stir into the cooked turkey and serve immediately.

SERVES 2.

Seafood

A friend of mine came over the other day and said he had something important to tell me. We have shared a lot, he and I: hangovers, broken hearts, and many a large piece of barbecued meat. I sat and wondered, while he bumbled. Finally, awkwardly, he stumbled it out: "James, I've met this woman, and I've become an ichthyophagist." ■ I was stunned. I had to be supportive, after all, he was my friend, but what the hell was he admitting to? I made a few sympathetic noises and excused myself to sneak off for a dictionary. ■ Ichthyophagy is the act of eating fish—lots of fish—and my friend, you must understand, is a butcher by trade and a meat eater by avocation. He has spent his life surrounded by meat, and suddenly, out of his closet, he was in love with fish. He told me first because I share his passion. ■ My love affair with seafood began like so many others'— with a simple plate of fish and chips brought home in newspaper by my father. I will never forget the taste of that first time. As I got older my interest deepened. Many nights found me combing the darker streets of London in search of interesting fish dishes. Often, out of desperation, I smuggled my fish and chips upstairs to

my room in a plain brown wrapper. My mother, it seemed, was always serving lamb. She just didn't understand. . . . ■ Adult life and travel added glamour to my passion. I hit the fish markets in strange cities rather than the bars, and all over the world I chased the exotic textures and flavours of seafood. I ate fresh swordfish on the shores of Turkey, clams no bigger than my thumbnail in Italy, giant red lobsters in Nova Scotia, and in Japan, not just raw tuna but once, at a kite-flying dinner, small live goldfish which wriggled for at least five minutes before I dared unclench my back teeth. By then I knew there was no turning back. ■ The years that followed deepened my understanding and appreciation. Although I never understood it, I came to forgive those who didn't share my passion for seafood. Perhaps they had never truly tasted ecstasy. Maybe I am just more at peace now. I live in a waterfront city where what isn't caught can be flown in from anywhere. My days of combing the back streets are over. The community is supportive, the food is fantastic, and I have finally found a lady-love who sells fish. ■

Steamed Scallops

There are many ways of steaming. Either use a wok or frypan and place a Chinese bamboo steamer and lid inside. Or use one of those collapsible stainless-steel steamers in a deep frypan with lid. Or use a steamer saucepan set. . . . Basically, you use what you've got or improvise!

INGREDIENTS

3 Tbsp/45 mL rice vinegar*
  (or white wine vinegar)
1 slice fresh ginger
6–8 scallops in the shell
2 slices fresh ginger, julienned
1 green onion, shredded

2 star anise* (or ½ tsp/2.5 mL fennel seed)
1 piece orange peel
1 cup/250 mL water
2 cloves garlic, slivered
Small handful Chinese preserved black beans*
Few drops soy sauce

Put the vinegar, star anise, orange peel, ginger and water in the bottom half of your steamer and bring to the boil. Turn down the heat slightly and put the scallops and remaining ingredients in the top half of your steamer. Cover securely and steam for 3 to 4 minutes.

*Available at Oriental markets and some supermarkets.   SERVES 2.

Salmon Baked on Cedar

A slight variation of the authentic Canadian west coast Native custom. Atlantic salmon works just as well, but with different results. *(See illustration facing page 64.)*

INGREDIENTS

1 salmon fillet (1–2 lbs/500 g–1 kg)
Juice of 1 lemon
1 Tbsp/15 mL chopped
  fresh basil (or 1 tsp/5 mL dried)

⅓ cup/80 mL olive oil
Zest of 1 lemon
Salt & pepper

Preheat oven to 450°F/220°C.

Marinate the salmon in the oil, lemon, basil, salt and pepper for at least 20 minutes. Meanwhile, soak a cedar plank (untreated) in cold water for about 10 minutes. Remove and bake the plank for 5 to 10 minutes.

Remove the salmon from the marinade and bake on the plank until cooked—about 8 minutes per finger thickness of fish.

      SERVES 2.

Mission Hill Salmon

This is melt-in-your-mouth food.

INGREDIENTS

2 Tbsp/30 mL butter

1 cup/250 mL dry white wine

2 green onions, chopped

Juice of ½ lemon

1 Tbsp/15 mL honey

Salt & pepper

2 salmon steaks

2 Tbsp/30 mL chopped fresh parsley

¼ cup/50 mL yoghurt or light cream

2 Tbsp/30 mL Dijon mustard

½ tsp/2.5 mL tarragon

Melt the butter in a large frypan over medium heat and sear the salmon steaks for 1 minute on each side. Add ½ cup/125 mL wine, parsley and onions, cover and cook for 5 to 6 minutes.

Remove the salmon to a warmed plate, turn up the heat and add the rest of the ingredients. Stir for 1 to 2 minutes or until the sauce has thickened and pour over the salmon.

SERVES 2.

Grilled Salmon & Wilted Spinach

Popeye's favourite!

INGREDIENTS

2 salmon steaks

1 Tbsp/15 mL Olive Oil (She
   had to make it into this recipe.)

1 bunch fresh spinach, washed
   (or 1 packet frozen, thawed)

Juice of ½ lime

1 Tbsp/15 mL soy sauce

1 Tbsp/15 mL sesame oil

2 Tbsp/30 mL sesame seeds

Marinate the salmon steaks in the lime juice, Olive Oil, soy sauce and sesame oil for at least half an hour.

Heat a dry frypan, lightly toast the sesame seeds and set them aside.

Remove the steaks from the marinade and broil for about 5 minutes each side.

Meanwhile, steam the spinach lightly, drain and arrange on a plate. Place the salmon steaks on top and sprinkle with toasted sesame seeds.

SERVES 2.

Shrimp, Rosemary & Garlic Kebabs

Very pretty barbecue fare.

INGREDIENTS

3 Tbsp/45 mL butter	*1 Tbsp/15 mL pepper*
1 Tbsp/15 mL rosemary, chopped	*6 cloves garlic, finely chopped*
Juice of 1 lemon	*1 tsp/5 mL cayenne pepper*
15 large shrimp or prawns	*1 zucchini, cut into large cubes*
Fresh rosemary sprigs (or watercress)	

Melt the butter, pepper and chopped rosemary in a saucepan, then add and gently heat the garlic, lemon juice and cayenne pepper.

Thread the shrimp and zucchini onto wooden skewers, brush with the butter sauce and grill for 2 minutes each side, brushing with more butter sauce.

Serve on a platter of fresh rosemary sprigs (or watercress).

SERVES 2.

Fried Prawns & Mango Salad

Another beautiful dish filled with different taste sensations. *(See illustration on overleaf facing page 64.)*

INGREDIENTS

Vegetable oil	*1 Tbsp/15 mL peppercorns*
1½ lbs/750 g whole, unpeeled prawns	*½ tsp/2.5 mL salt*
1 Tbsp/15 mL grated fresh ginger	*2 mangoes, peeled & cubed*
Spinach leaves	*Lettuce leaves*
Juice of a lemon	*Freshly ground black pepper*

Pour ½ in/1 cm of oil into a medium-sized saucepan and heat with the peppercorns until sizzling. Quickly fry the prawns for about 1 or 2 minutes, drain, dry them and toss in a mixture of salt and grated ginger.

Mix with the mango cubes and pile onto a plate of spinach and lettuce leaves. Squeeze lemon juice over the top and sprinkle with freshly ground black pepper.

SERVES 4 FOR A STARTER OR 2 FOR A MAIN COURSE.

Salmon in Filo Pastry

(**fee**-lo)

You won't feel low with this dish!

INGREDIENTS

4 sheets filo pastry*

2 Tbsp/30 mL toasted sesame seeds

1 tsp/5 mL brown sugar

1 Tbsp/15 mL fresh dill, chopped

Salt & pepper

2 Tbsp/30 mL butter

1 salmon fillet (¾–1 lb/375–500 g), halved

½ onion, finely chopped

Juice of ½ orange

Preheat oven to 400°F/200°C.

Unwrap the filo pastry and keep covered with a damp towel. Melt the butter in a small saucepan. Brush one sheet of filo with butter and sprinkle with some sesame seeds. Cover with another sheet and repeat the procedure until you have 4 sheets stacked up.

Cut in half and lay a salmon piece on each half. Sprinkle each salmon piece with brown sugar, onion, dill, orange juice, salt and pepper. Draw up the edges around the fish and pinch into a drawstring bag. Brush with more butter and sesame seeds and bake for 20 minutes.

*Available in the frozen-foods section of most
supermarkets and some Greek bakeries.

SERVES 2.

Halibut with Mango Mayonnaise

A blissfully happy marriage of ingredients.

INGREDIENTS

2 halibut steaks

4 slices fresh ginger, thinly sliced

½ cup/125 mL fresh lime juice

2 Tbsp/30 mL vegetable oil

Marinate the halibut steaks in the lime juice and ginger for at least 30 minutes. Remove from the marinade, heat the oil in a frypan over high heat and cook the steaks for 7 to 8 minutes per finger thickness of fish. Serve with Mango Mayonnaise.

MANGO MAYONNAISE

2 eggs

½ tsp/2.5 mL pepper

Juice of 1 lime

1 mango, peeled

¼ tsp/1 mL salt

1 tsp/5 mL mustard

½ cup/125 mL vegetable oil

Beat the eggs, salt, pepper, mustard and lime juice together in a food processor or blender on medium speed. Slowly add the oil in a steady stream, beating constantly until thick. Add the mango, blend further until smooth and serve with the halibut.

SERVES 2.

Salmon with Rhubarb & Rice Stuffing

What to do with all that rhubarb growing out back! Rhubarb adds a nice tang to the stuffing— a real gourmet touch without the expense. Try the stuffing with chicken instead.

INGREDIENTS

2 Tbsp/30 mL butter
Salt & pepper

2 salmon steaks

STUFFING

1 cup/250 mL chopped rhubarb
1 stick celery, finely chopped
1 egg, beaten
½ tsp/2.5 mL basil

3 green onions, finely chopped
1 cup/250 mL cooked rice
1 tsp/5 mL brown sugar
Fresh basil leaves

Melt 1 Tbsp/15 mL butter in a fry-pan over medium heat, sprinkle the salmon steaks with salt and pepper and fry for 8 minutes per finger thickness of fish, turning once.

Meanwhile, melt the other 1 Tbsp/15 mL butter in a large saucepan and sauté the rhubarb, onion and celery until softened, about 5 to 10 minutes. Stir in the rest of the ingredients, reserving the basil leaves, and heat through.

Make a bed of the stuffing on a plate and lay the salmon steaks on top. Decorate with fresh basil leaves.

SERVES 2.

> **Wine makes daily living easier, less hurried, with fewer tensions and more tolerance. —Benjamin Franklin**

Barbecued Sausages & Oysters

The Odd Couple! These two actually get along well.

INGREDIENTS

1 cup/250 mL soy sauce	1 cup/250 mL brown sugar
1 cup/250 mL vinegar	1 Tbsp/15 mL cornstarch
2–3 Tbsp/30–45 mL whiskey	¼ tsp/1 mL cayenne pepper
½ tsp/2.5 mL paprika	8 thick sausages
8 oysters, shucked	Watercress or fresh spinach leaves

Bring the soy sauce, sugar and vinegar to a boil in a medium-sized saucepan, stirring well. Mix the cornstarch and enough whiskey together to make a paste and stir into the soy sauce mixture. Turn down the heat and add the cayenne pepper and paprika. Stir until the mixture is thick and glossy and remove from the heat.

Brush sausages with this sauce and grill on a hot rack, basting with more sauce, for about 10 minutes. Brush the oysters with sauce and grill with the sausages for about 5 minutes, basting with extra sauce if necessary. Serve on a bed of watercress or fresh spinach leaves.

If you don't have a barbecue, fry the sausages and oysters or bake them in a 400°F/200°C oven, allowing 25 to 30 minutes for the sausages and 5 minutes for the oysters.

SERVES 4.

Steamed Trout with Black Beans

Rainbow trout still glistening with lake water are the best but, in a pinch, farm-raised trout still deliver a great taste.

INGREDIENTS

2 small fresh trout	2 green onions
2 Tbsp/30 mL soy sauce	2 Tbsp/30 mL sherry
2 tsp/10 mL sugar	1 clove garlic, finely chopped
1 Tbsp/15 mL vegetable oil	1 Tbsp/15 mL Chinese preserved black beans*

Slash each side of the trouts diagonally. Slice the green onion diagonally and mix with the soy, sherry, sugar, garlic and oil. Marinate the trout in this mixture for 20 minutes.

Place the trout on a plate or lettuce leaf in the steamer, scatter the remaining marinade and the black beans over the fish, cover securely and steam for about 8 to 10 minutes.

*Available at Oriental markets.

SERVES 2.

Steamed Trout with Black Beans & the Whole Shebang

Try this meal-in-one by steaming the trout as above with accompanying vegetables using a Chinese bamboo three-tier steamer. Get the timing right. . . . Put the potatoes in first, add the trout after about 2 minutes and add the asparagus after about 8 minutes.

Place small, new potatoes in the bottom section of the steamer. Sprinkle with salt and chopped mint and steam for a total of 10 minutes.

Place the trout in the middle section and steam for a total of 8 to 10 minutes.

Place a bunch of asparagus (stringy ends removed) in the upper section, sprinkle with salt and steam for a total of 2 to 3 minutes.

Arrange the asparagus as a mat on the plate. Lay the fish on top and the potatoes around. Scatter sliced green onion on top.

SERVES 1 OR 2.

Tomatoes, Lima Beans & Clams

I hated lima beans as a kid. It took me years to try them again. What a pleasant surprise.

INGREDIENTS

1 Tbsp/15 mL oil	1 Tbsp/15 mL butter
1 onion, chopped	3 slices fresh ginger, julienned
1 cup/250 mL cherry tomatoes	2 cloves garlic, chopped
Salt & pepper	1 glass white wine
2 cups/500 mL lima	2 Tbsp/30 mL fresh mint, chopped
beans, fresh or frozen	4 cups small fresh clams, scrubbed

Heat the oil and butter in a large saucepan over medium heat. Sauté the onion and ginger, stirring well, and add the tomatoes, garlic, salt and pepper. Pour in the wine, add the lima beans and chopped mint and arrange the clams on top.

Cover and cook until the clams open, about 6 minutes. Discard any clams that haven't opened. Serve on a large platter with crusty bread and garnish with more chopped fresh mint.

SERVES 2.

Moules Marinière

(**mool** mare-in-**yare**)

This is one of my favourite dishes to serve for an informal dinner party. I dump a great whack of mussels onto a large platter and let people dig in. Add a good loaf of crusty bread, a green salad and maybe a nice bottle of white wine. Dead easy.

INGREDIENTS

1 Tbsp/15 mL butter or vegetable oil

2 glasses white wine or water
    with juice and zest of 2 lemons

Zest of ½ orange

4 cups fresh mussels (in their
    shells), washed & scrubbed

2 shallots or ½ onion, finely chopped

3 cloves garlic, finely chopped

Salt & pepper

½ tsp/2.5 mL thyme

3 Tbsp/45 mL parsley, chopped

Heat the butter or oil in a large deep-sided frypan over medium heat and cook the shallots until softened. Pour in the wine, add the garlic, salt, pepper, orange zest, thyme and mussels. Cover and bring to the boil.

Simmer for 1 to 2 minutes, or until the mussels open. (Discard any that do not open.) Tip onto a platter and top with parsley. Serve with crusty bread to sop up the garlicky juices.

SERVES 2.

Clams & Scallops Marinière

INGREDIENTS

1 Tbsp/15 mL butter or vegetable oil

½ bottle cider

4 slices ginger, julienned

2 cups/500 mL fresh clams (in their
    shells), washed & scrubbed

2 cups/500 mL fresh scallops (in
    their shells), washed

2 shallots or ½ onion, finely chopped

3 cloves garlic, finely chopped

Zest of ½ lemon

Salt & pepper

3 Tbsp/45 mL parsley, chopped

Heat the butter in a large deep-sided frypan and cook the shallots until softened. Add the cider, garlic, ginger, lemon zest, salt, pepper, clams and scallops. Cover and bring to the boil.

Simmer for 1 to 2 minutes, or until the clam and scallop shells are open. (Discard any that do not open.) Tip onto a large platter, scatter with chopped parsley and serve with crusty bread and a great salad.

SERVES 2.

Buttered Crab

Just because a recipe is ridiculously simple and straightforward doesn't mean it's not good.

INGREDIENTS

- 1 Tbsp/15 mL butter
- 1 bunch parsley, chopped
- 1 Tbsp/15 mL breadcrumbs
- 1 Tbsp/15 mL sherry
- ¼ lb/125 g crabmeat (fresh or canned)
- Juice of 1 lemon
- 1 Tbsp/15 mL black pepper
- Pinch of salt

Melt the butter in a frypan or saucepan over medium heat and stir in all the rest of the ingredients. Cook, stirring, for 2 to 3 minutes until creamy and serve on buttered toast.

SERVES 2.

Crab & Ginger

Buy a live crab and keep it loosely wrapped in an open plastic or paper bag in the fridge or on ice. Don't put it in tap water or it'll die.

Bring a large saucepan of salted water to the boil. Add the crab, cover and simmer for 20 minutes. Remove the crab, drain, and cut the legs and body into pieces.

INGREDIENTS

- 2 Tbsp/30 mL vegetable oil
- 3 slices ginger, finely chopped
- 1 cooked crab, cut into
  pieces (see above)
- 1 Tbsp/15 mL sherry
- 1 onion, cut into chunks
- 2 Tbsp/30 mL freshly ground black pepper
- 3 green onions, cut into lengths
- 1 tsp/5 mL cornstarch
- 2–3 Tbsp/30–45 mL cilantro, chopped

Heat the oil in a wok or large frypan and sauté the onions over high heat. Add the ginger and pepper and stir well. Add the crab pieces and green onions and stir until everything is well coated.

Mix the cornstarch and sherry into a paste and stir into the wok to glaze the mixture lightly. Serve over rice and garnish with chopped cilantro.

SERVES 2.

Salmon & Miso

(**mee**-SO)

Of the endless ways to serve salmon, this is one of my favourites. Not too heavy and with lots of complex flavours.

INGREDIENTS

4 Tbsp/60 mL miso paste*

1 Tbsp/15 mL honey

1 clove garlic, chopped

2 salmon steaks

1 tsp/5 mL sugar

½ tsp/2.5 mL ginger powder

2 Tbsp/30 mL white wine or apple juice

Mix all ingredients except salmon in a small bowl and brush onto the salmon steaks. Heat a dry frypan over high heat and fry the steaks for 8 minutes per finger thickness of fish, turning once.

*Available at Japanese markets.

SERVES 2.

Fish & Prawn Casserole with Coconut

The coconut makes this dish just a little bit exotic.

INGREDIENTS

1 lb/500 g white fish fillets, cut into pieces

3 Tbsp/45 mL flour

1 onion, chopped

1 parsnip, grated

2 whole, red chilis

Salt & pepper

1 lb/500 g prawns

1 can (14 oz/398 mL) coconut milk*

1 carrot, grated

1 tomato, chopped

2–3 Tbsp/30–45 mL grated
coconut (unsweetened)

Preheat oven to 400°F/200°C.

Shake the fish, prawns and flour in a plastic bag and remove the lightly coated pieces.

Pour ⅓ can of coconut milk into a large frypan and heat over medium heat. (Do not boil.) Add the fish, prawns and onions and poach for 2 to 3 minutes.

Tip into a medium-sized baking dish and add the carrot, tomato, parsnip and chilis. Season with salt and pepper, add the rest of the coconut milk and dot with grated coconut. Bake for 15 minutes.

*Available at Oriental markets and most supermarkets.

SERVES 4.

Salmon Baked on Cedar *(see recipe on page 55)*

Fried Prawns & Mango Salad *(see recipe on page 57)*

Frijoles Negros *(see recipe on page 105)*

Polenta Quattro Formaggio *(see recipe on page 104)*

Huachinango Veracruz

(wa-**chin**-ain-go)

A Mexican classic with a nice bite that complements rather than overwhelms the delicate flavour of the fish. Don't let the name scare you; this is a snap to make.

INGREDIENTS

2 Tbsp/30 mL vegetable oil

2–3 cloves garlic, finely chopped

1 cup/250 mL chopped
  tomatoes, fresh or canned

1 red snapper fillet or other firm
  white fish (¾ lb/375 g), halved

1 onion, chopped

1 fresh chili pepper, chopped

Juice of ½ lime

¼ tsp/1 mL cinnamon

Salt & pepper

3 Tbsp/45 mL fresh chopped cilantro

Heat the oil in a large frypan over high heat and sauté the onion, garlic and chili pepper until softened. Stir in the tomatoes and allow to stew for 5 minutes.

Lay in the snapper fillets, sprinkle with lime juice, cinnamon, salt and pepper. Cover and simmer for 7 to 8 minutes. Arrange on plates and garnish with chopped cilantro.

SERVES 2.

Indonesian Fish

Mild and sweet, this is a perfect start for those who are a little frightened of curry.

INGREDIENTS

4 Tbsp/60 mL grated coconut

Salt & pepper

2 eggs, beaten

2 bananas, peeled, halved & then
  halved again lengthwise

1 Tbsp/15 mL curry powder

4 sole fillets or any white fish (¾ lb/375 g)

4 Tbsp/60 mL oil

Lemon wedges

Mix the coconut, curry powder, salt and pepper together in a flat dish. Dip each fish fillet in the egg and then the coconut mixture.

Heat the oil in a frypan over medium-high heat and sauté the fish on both sides until lightly browned (2 to 3 minutes each side).

Remove to a warmed plate, add a little extra oil to the frypan if necessary and sauté the bananas quickly on both sides. Arrange around the fish and serve with lemon wedges.

SERVES 2.

Smelts Escabèche

(ess-ka-**besh**)

Smelts seem to be a sadly forgotten fish. If you haven't had them before, they're certainly worth a try. They have a good meaty taste. Just watch the bones.

INGREDIENTS

½ lb/250 g smelts

2–3 Tbsp/30–45 mL oil

1 small, red bell pepper, diced

1 red hot pepper, finely chopped or
  ½ tsp/2.5 mL dried chili flakes

Salt & pepper

3–4 Tbsp/45–60 mL flour

½ onion, minced

2–3 Tbsp/30–45 mL olive oil

1 Tbsp/15 mL wine vinegar

1 tsp/5 mL oregano

Shake the smelts and flour together in a plastic bag until the smelts are finely covered. Remove. Heat the oil in a large frypan over high heat and fry the smelts until lightly browned.

Arrange them in a medium-sized shallow dish. Sprinkle over them the onion, red pepper, olive oil, vinegar, hot pepper, oregano, salt and pepper, cover and leave to pickle overnight in the fridge. Eat them cold with a good rye bread and bottle of beer!

**SERVES 2 AS MAIN COURSE
OR 4 AS AN APPETIZER.**

Pork

When Louise inherited the pig farm she wasn't sure that it was such a blessing. There she was, alone, out of work and in desperate need of *something;* still she never expected that her sweet but eccentric uncle would confer such dubious honor upon her. After all, what did she know about farming? But for all this, Louise was a sensible woman. Despite her complete ignorance, she made the best of a bad job and packed up her house, her cat, and her Elvis memorabilia collection and moved on down to the "piggery." Little did she know it would change her life. ■ Louise knew that her Uncle was a bit crazy, but what she found still amazed her. Everywhere there were pictures of pigs, framed quotations about pigs, art about pigs, *everywhere* pigs, pigs, and more pigs. As she tacked her life-sized poster of Elvis in Memphis to the largest wall she could find, she reflected that maybe her uncle had been a little too obsessed. ■ By day, Louise worked in the barn. She grew to love the pigs' little bouncy personalities and happy ways. By night, she cooked lots of pork dishes and read all her Uncle's pig books and learned everything she needed to know to be a success as a pig farmer. Little by little, Louise came to know what pigs were all about. ■ Little by little, Louise also came to pity the poor little beasts. She read about pigs in China and Vietnam, where their plumpness and fertility make them a symbol of wealth and abundance, but it seemed the rest of the world had banished the pig to the bottom of the social ladder. She became painfully aware that even the smallest child knows that a "pig" is a greedy and undesirable person. Pigs, according to contemporary folk wisdom, are indiscriminate in their eating habits, and suggested the even worse cultural evils of lust, egotism, stupidity and extravagance. Even the Bible, where Louise sometimes went for guidance, tells the parable of pearls before swine in which it portrays pigs as ignorant and unworthy. To make matters worse, pigs are traditionally fatty little scavengers, making them decidedly unpopular with food snobs. Oh, and let us not forget the pigs' legendary love of mud. . . . ■ Now the pig is an ancient and honourable animal, and the more she thought about this, the more distressed Louise became about their bad reputation. She knew, because she raised them, that her pigs were sanitary, well mannered, and not at all stupid. She knew, because she cooked them, that her pigs were delicious, nutri-

tious and lean. Something had to be done, but what? ■ One day, it hit Louise (the idea, that is, not the plaster bust of Elvis that she kept over the bed) that she should start a Friends of the Pig society and spend the rest of her life lobbying for pig awareness all over the world. The society was a hit, and the rest of Louise's history is, well, history. Suffice it to say that she replaced old Elvis with yet more pig pictures, she found herself a man who loved pigs as much as she did, and she became a very rich and powerful woman. ■

Pork Tenderloin & Red Currant Sauce

Pork is one of my favourite meats. This recipe really enhances its robust flavour. To butterfly pork tenderloin, slice along the length of the meat without cutting completely through, and then open it out.

INGREDIENTS

Juice of ½ lemon

2 cloves garlic, crushed

2 Tbsp/30 mL Dijon mustard

2 Tbsp/30 mL light soy sauce

¼ cup/50 mL olive oil

1 Tbsp/15 mL honey

1 tsp/5 mL chili powder

1 pork tenderloin (1 lb/500 g), butterflied & sliced

Mix all the ingredients together in a bowl and marinate the pork slices for at least 1 hour. Remove the slices from the marinade and fry in a dry, hot frypan until brown on each side (1 to 2 minutes). Serve with Red Currant Sauce.

RED CURRANT SAUCE

½ cup/125 mL red currant jam

1 tsp/5 mL red wine vinegar

1 Tbsp/15 mL Dijon mustard

Salt & pepper to taste

Melt the jam in a small saucepan over medium heat and stir in the mustard. Just before serving, stir in the vinegar, salt and pepper.

SERVES 4.

Rolled Pork & Asparagus

This is a pretty little dish that looks like it took a lot of work. Mirin is a Japanese sweetened rice wine used in salad dressings, dipping sauces, stews and marinades and is part of the glaze in teriyaki dishes.

INGREDIENTS

8 very thin pork tenderloin
   slices (approx. ½ lb/250 g)

1 Tbsp/15 mL sake*

1 Tbsp/15 mL vegetable oil

3 Tbsp/45 mL soy sauce

1 Tbsp/15 mL sugar

2 Tbsp/30 mL mirin*

8 asparagus spears, stringy ends removed

Marinate the pork in the soy, sugar, sake and mirin for 20 minutes.

Steam the asparagus for 2 to 3 minutes and halve. Remove the pork from the marinade, pat dry and lay 2 asparagus halves in the centre of each slice (asparagus should show at each end). Secure with toothpicks if necessary.

Heat 1 Tbsp/15 mL vegetable oil in a frypan over medium-high heat and fry the pork parcels for 2 to 3 minutes. Arrange on a platter.

*Available in Japanese markets and specialty liquor stores.   SERVES 2.

Pork Stew Like You've Never Tasted

This is a lovely combination of flavours. The tomatillos add an interesting tartness as the fruit sweetens. This can be cooked in the oven or entirely on the stove top.

INGREDIENTS

2 Tbsp/30 mL olive oil	1 lb/500 g boneless pork loin, cubed
1 onion, chopped	½ cup/125 mL peanuts or walnuts
3 green tomatoes or tomatillos*	2 cloves garlic
3 chili peppers	½ cup/125 mL stock or apple juice
Handful of chopped fresh cilantro	2 apples, cored & sliced
2 pears, cored & sliced	2 bananas, peeled & sliced
1 cup/250 mL frozen peas	1 can (14 oz/398 mL) corn

If using the oven, preheat to 375°F/190°C.

Heat the oil in a large, deep-sided frypan and sauté the pork until brown. Add the onion and peanuts and brown. Chop the tomatoes and add to the pan with the garlic and chili peppers. Pour in the stock or apple juice and sprinkle with chopped cilantro.

Arrange the apples, pears, bananas, peas and corn on top of the pork, cover and cook for 20 minutes.

Alternatively, tip into a casserole, cover and bake for 20 to 30 minutes.

*Available in   SERVES 4.
Mexican markets.

> **Thyme dates back to ancient Greece, where it was regarded as a symbol of courage and burned as incense by the Romans.**

Pork & Leek Stove-Top Casserole

Slightly sweet and almost rich.

INGREDIENTS

1 lb/500 g pork tenderloin, cubed
1 tsp/5 mL pepper
1 Tbsp/15 mL butter
3 leeks, chopped
1 glass white wine
Salt & pepper
1 tsp/5 mL fresh thyme
1 cup/250 mL small mushrooms
Fresh chive flowers, if available

3-4 Tbsp/45–60 mL flour
1 Tbsp/15 mL olive oil
1 large onion, chopped
4 whole cloves garlic
1 glass stock or apple juice or water
1 tsp/5 mL Dijon mustard
1 tsp/5 mL fresh lavender (optional)
¼ cup/50 mL light cream

Shake the pork cubes, flour and pepper in a plastic bag and remove the lightly dusted meat. Heat the oil in a large deep-sided frypan over high heat and sauté the pork until lightly browned.

Melt the butter in the pan and add the onion, leeks and garlic and stir well until lightly browned. Pour in the wine and stock and add the salt, pepper, mustard, thyme and lavender. Simmer for 5 to 10 minutes or until pork is well done, then add the mushrooms and stir in the cream until heated through.

Decorate with chive flowers or lavender and serve with thick slices of crusty French bread.

SERVES 4.

Grunt Mushrooms

These mushrooms were not happy to be picked . . . hence the name.

INGREDIENTS

2 Tbsp/30 mL oil

2 cups/500 mL small
   mushrooms, whole

½ tsp/2.5 mL salt

2 Tbsp/30 mL vinegar

1 bay leaf

1 bottle beer (or substitute apple juice)

1 onion, chopped

2 tomatoes, chopped

3 cloves garlic, chopped

1 tsp/5 mL pepper

1 tsp/5 mL caraway seeds

¾ lb/375 g garlic sausage, sliced thickly

Heat the oil in a frypan and fry the onion until softened. Add the rest of the ingredients, except the beer, and stir together for 2 to 3 minutes. Pour in the beer, cover and simmer for 10 minutes. Stir until liquid is thick.

Tastes even better the next day. Serve with a good loaf of sourdough bread.

SERVES 4.

Pork & Pineapple

An updated (and much improved) version of the Hawaiian pork recipes so popular in the '60s.

INGREDIENTS

2 Tbsp/30 mL coconut milk

½ tsp/2.5 mL salt

1 onion, finely chopped

1 red bell pepper, julienned

1 cup/250 mL chopped pineapple

1 tsp/5 mL cornstarch

3 Tbsp/45 mL fresh cilantro, chopped

1 lb/500 g pork tenderloin, cubed

1 tsp/5 mL black pepper

1 tsp/5 mL turmeric

1 green bell pepper, julienned

3 whole chili peppers

½ cup/125 mL pineapple juice

Heat the coconut milk in a frypan and sauté the meat until slightly coloured, about 2 to 3 minutes. Sprinkle with salt and pepper and add the onion and turmeric. Cook for about 2 to 3 minutes. Stir in the red and green peppers, chopped pineapple and chili peppers.

Mix the cornstarch with pineapple juice and stir into the mixture. Cook for 4 to 5 minutes or until the pork is thoroughly cooked.

Serve with chopped cilantro over rice.

SERVES 4.

Lamb

Every spring the locals of Saturna Island celebrate spring with a good old-fashioned pagan lamb bake. By daybreak a giant 15-foot pit is filled with a roaring and crackling fire, and then circled by 20 butchered and dressed lambs which will stand cooking around the perimeter for the entire day. Six hundred people come to celebrate. Families with strollers, business-men in jogging suits, young lovers on bicycles, and grandmothers on tractors. All around the sizzling lamb, feet run races, faces get painted, large rough hands play tug-of-war, fingers play guitars, and beautiful boats sail into the harbour. ■ After a day of hard fun and games played out to the increasingly enticing smell of wood smoke and roasting lamb, the final awaited taste is bliss on a fork. Cooked by good simple folk in a good simple way and seasoned with fresh air, sunshine, smiles and anticipation, the flavour of the meat explodes on your taste buds like daffodils on a hillside. ■ The truth is, lamb tastes pretty wonderful no matter what you do to it. It is really *hard* to screw up. Curried, baked, stewed, fried, or even thrown on the barbey and over-cooked, the flavour of lamb is still rich and sweet and delicious. In the un-likely event that you have leftovers, cold lamb is as good as any candy. ■ Buy fresh lamb if you can get it, but New Zealand lamb is good too. Little chops are pretty and elegant, or ask your butcher to bone a leg and you've got lots of lean meat and the bones for soup. (Despite what your grandmother told you, lamb broth is better than chicken soup for a day in bed with the flu.) Cheap cuts are good too—whip up a little Lamb Korma and your beloveds will call you the best damn lamb cook this side of the island roasting pit. ■ So go ahead—throw yourself a lamb festival. You may want to think carefully about whether or not you have room for tug-of-wars and egg races round the kitchen table, and your neighbours might prefer that you not build a 15-foot fire pit on the front lawn, but you can cook up a taste just as memorable. ■

Lamb Korma

I like curry a lot. It opens up endless possibilities in your cooking repertoire. And it's one of those dishes that get better the second day when the flavours start to meld. For lamb korma, if you think of it in advance, it's not a bad idea to marinate the lamb in the yoghurt for a few hours before cooking.

INGREDIENTS

1 Tbsp/15 mL butter

1 onion, chopped

Fresh ginger

¾ cup/175 mL yoghurt

Pinch saffron (soaked in hot water)

¼ cup/50 mL ground almonds

½ lb/250 g boned lamb, finely chopped

2 cloves garlic, chopped

Salt & pepper to taste

1 Tbsp/15 mL chopped chives

4 cardamom pods, crushed

Juice of 2 limes or lemons

Melt the butter and brown the lamb. Stir in the onions and brown also. Add the garlic, ginger, salt and pepper and pour in half the yoghurt. Stir in the rest of the ingredients, cover and simmer 20 minutes.

SERVES 2.

Breaded Lamb Cutlets

Mashed potatoes and peas (fresh please) kind of food.

INGREDIENTS

Brown breadcrumbs

6 lamb cutlets, trimmed

1 Tbsp/15 mL butter

Salt & pepper to taste

2 egg yolks, beaten

2 Tbsp/30 mL oil

Mix the breadcrumbs, salt and pepper together in a bowl. Dip each cutlet in egg and then breadcrumbs. (If you want to get fancy, smear each cutlet with mango chutney before dipping in egg). Leave to dry for about 1 hour.

Heat the butter and oil in a frypan and sauté the cutlets 4 minutes each side. Pile a mound of mashed potatoes onto a platter and arrange the cutlets on top like a crown.

SERVES 2.

Lamb Chops in Foil

The fragrance of these little parcels when they're broken open is terrific.

INGREDIENTS

1 tsp/5 mL Dijon mustard

¼ cup/50 mL fresh mint, chopped

Salt & pepper

½ lb/250 g mushrooms, sliced

Lemon juice

1 clove garlic, chopped

¼ cup/50 mL fresh parsley, chopped

2 thick lamb loin chops

2 Tbsp/30 mL butter

Preheat oven to 400°F/200°C.

Mix the mustard, garlic, mint, parsley, salt and pepper into a paste and coat both sides of the lamb chops with it. Cut 2 squares of aluminum foil (12 in/30 cm) and place a chop on each one.

Rub the mushrooms and butter together and arrange them over the chops. Seal the foil and bake for 20 minutes, then open and sprinkle with lemon juice. Serve in the parcels.

SERVES 2.

Lamb & Eggplant Salad

For those odd times you have leftover lamb.

INGREDIENTS

4 Tbsp/60 mL olive oil

2 cups/500 mL cooked lamb,
    thinly sliced

Fresh spinach leaves

1 eggplant, cubed

½ cup/125 mL black olives

2 tomatoes, chopped

Heat the oil and sauté the eggplant until tender. Drain. Mix with the lamb, olives and tomatoes and arrange over the spinach leaves. Serve with Yoghurt Dressing.

YOGHURT DRESSING

¼ cup/50 mL olive oil

Juice of ½ lemon

1 tsp/5 mL honey

Salt & pepper

2 Tbsp/30 mL yoghurt

3 cloves garlic, chopped

1 tsp/5 mL oregano

Mix all ingredients together by hand or in a blender.

SERVES 4.

Curried Goat—But We'll Use Lamb

A simple delicious curry.

INGREDIENTS

*½ lb/250 g boneless lamb, cut
    into bite-sized pieces*
1 onion, finely chopped
3 slices fresh ginger
1 tsp/5 mL ground cumin
1 cup/250 mL stock
4 green onions, finely chopped

2 Tbsp/30 mL flour
2 Tbsp/30 mL oil
4 cloves garlic, finely chopped
1 Tbsp/15 mL curry powder
1 whole chili pepper
Juice of a lime

Dust the lamb with flour. Heat the oil in a frypan and brown the meat. Keeping the heat up high, add the onions, garlic and ginger. Stir in the curry powder and spices, cook until aromatic and pour in the stock and lime juice. Turn the heat down and simmer over low heat for 20 minutes.

Sprinkle with chopped green onion and serve on rice.

SERVES 2.

Lamb & Coffee

We were doing a show on coffee and I was racking my brain for one more dish and came up with this somewhat odd combination. A lucky discovery. The slight bitterness from the coffee makes it special.

INGREDIENTS

2 Tbsp/30 mL oil

1 onion, chopped

6 cloves garlic, chopped

2 Tbsp/30 mL instant coffee

2 Tbsp/30 mL vinegar

3 green onions, chopped

¾ lb/375 g boneless lamb, cubed

Freshly ground black pepper

1 Tbsp/15 mL tomato paste

1 Tbsp/15 mL brown sugar

1 tsp/5 mL ground cumin

Zest of 1 orange

Heat the oil in a frypan over high heat and sauté the lamb pieces until lightly browned on both sides. Stir in the onion, pepper and garlic. Add the tomato paste and coffee and stir well. Add the sugar, vinegar and cumin, lower the heat to medium and simmer for 10 minutes.

Serve with chopped green onions and orange zest.

SERVES 2.

Lamb Kidney & Celery

My executive producer won't even walk into the studio when I'm cooking kidney or liver or any such thing. I think it has something to do with having to sit at the table as a child until she ate it. She doesn't know what she's missing.

INGREDIENTS

1 Tbsp/15 mL olive oil

6 whole cloves garlic

1 Tbsp/15 mL freshly ground pepper

6 lamb kidneys, thinly sliced

Juice of ½ orange

2 sticks celery, sliced diagonally

½ tsp/2.5 mL salt

Fresh rosemary

2 cups/500 mL quartered mushrooms

Heat the oil and sauté the celery slices and garlic. Sprinkle with salt, pepper and rosemary and stir in the kidney slices. Cook for 1 to 2 minutes and add the mushrooms.

Stir until softened, squeeze in the orange juice, stir well and serve immediately over noodles. Garnish with sprigs of fresh rosemary.

SERVES 3.

Beef

Back in the old days, when men was men, Miss Daisy sure knew how to cook, but it was Jake and Jedd who rounded up the herd. Cattle raisin' was men's work, and cattle eatin' was men's work too. Of course only the blue-eyed cowboys really knew how to do it. Them sheep-herders were wimps, and then, in the movies I saw, there were always them Spaniards with their curly mustachios and big black hats, and not one of them ever *understood* beef, 'cause every time they tried to get in on the action they seemed to get locked up by good ol' Sheriff Howdie. ■ We all believed in John Wayne and the beefsteak, the ropin,' the tyin' and the ky-y-yippee-i-in'. Beef was what made cowboys men, and what kept the west wild. Unfortunately, none of us had the sense to stop by the kitchen and check with Miss Daisy. She knew that the cowboy myth only really ex-isted in the movies, and the cowboy was no more than a little boys' fantasy pro-duced on film by a much bigger boy who himself wanted nothing more than to be-lieve. Miss Daisy tells it like this. . . . ■ "One fine day a Spanish ship sailed into the harbour carrying a fine herd of prime cattle. These Spanish were pretty clever. They

knew a whole lot more about good eatin' than we did, and they knew that white hats were silly because they showed the dirt. They also knew that there was a lot more to a cow than prime rib. Oxen (which are modified cows) were strong enough to pull wagons, and neither as expensive nor as temperamental as horses. Cows gave milk, and a quiet and placid life encouraged them to give even more, rather than being chased around by guys with guns. And milk meant marital bliss, with cake for dessert, corn flakes for breakfast and whipped cream with the strawberries. ■ And the Native folk, they knew better too. They knew more than a thing or two about riding around on horses in the great wild country, and they, like the Spaniards, also knew how to eat. They were the real 'cowboys.' They had the sense to see that you can't keep cows in New York City and drove the cattle over the Mississippi and onto the home where the buffalo roamed. ■ We eventually had the sense to see the sense in that, but no sooner had we learned than we set out to build a noisy ol' steel railway to drive the beef back to the East where it came from originally. Let me tell you, them was none too romantic times. ■ So it was the Spanish and the Natives who taught the rest of us how to do it. ■ Without them Jedd wouldn't have his jerky, Jake wouldn't have his Tex-Mex burger, and I'd be slinging drinks in the Gold Miner Saloon. As for Sheriff Howdie, he's only a lawman 'cause farmin' gives him asthma." ■ That's what Miss Daisy says. And the day she told me that story was the last day of my childhood. The movies have never been the same since. But in true western style Miss Daisy made me a man. She taught me about *real* western cooking. I learned about Six-Pak Stu, and I learned about Sweet and Sour Liver, and I learned about Hungarian beef and Chinese beef and all the wonderful things you can do with beef other than burn it on an open fire. ■

Sweet & Sour Liver

Just try it; you'll like it. The trick to liver is not to overcook it.

INGREDIENTS

Breadcrumbs   ½ tsp/2.5 mL salt
½ tsp/2.5 mL pepper   2 Tbsp/30 mL olive oil
1 lb/500 g calves' liver, thinly sliced   3 cloves garlic, finely chopped
1 Tbsp/15 mL sugar   2 Tbsp/30 mL wine vinegar

Season the breadcrumbs with salt and pepper. Heat 1 Tbsp/15 mL olive oil in a frypan over medium-high heat, dip the liver into the breadcrumbs and quickly sauté for 2 to 3 minutes. Remove.

Heat the rest of the olive oil and sauté the garlic and sugar until melted. Pour in the vinegar, stir and pour over the liver.

Serve with baby new potatoes and asparagus and garnish with mint.

SERVES 3.

Sesame Liver Strips

Don't cook liver too long; once it shrivels up, it starts to taste rancid.

INGREDIENTS

Sesame seeds   ½ tsp/2.5 mL cayenne pepper
¾ lb/375 g calves' liver   2 Tbsp/30 mL vinegar
1 Tbsp/15 mL sugar

Mix together the sesame seeds and cayenne pepper. Cut the liver into thin strips and dip into the sesame seeds. Heat a tablespoon or two of oil in a frypan over medium-high heat and lightly fry the strips until brown and crispy, about 2 minutes.

Add the vinegar and sugar, stir until the sugar has melted and serve hot.

SERVES 2.

Six-Pak Stu

Your favourite team might not win the game, but with this stu, you'll please those fans!

INGREDIENTS

1 lb/500 g stewing beef, cubed

2 Tbsp/30 mL butter

2 onions, chopped

1½ bottles beer

1 Tbsp/15 mL vinegar

1 bay leaf

½ tsp/2.5 mL basil

2 Tbsp/30 mL flour

2 Tbsp/30 mL oil

1 potato, diced

1½ tsp/7.5 mL sugar

1 clove garlic, chopped

1 tsp/5 mL thyme

Salt & pepper

Preheat oven to 350°F/180°C.

Place beef and flour in a plastic bag and shake until beef is lightly coated in flour. Remove. Melt the butter and oil in a large saucepan and brown the meat over high heat. Reduce heat and add the onions and potato and brown.

Add the rest of the ingredients, stir well and pour into a large casserole dish. Bake for 1½ to 2 hours.

If you want to cook it quicker, use cubes of pork tenderloin instead of stewing beef and cook as in the above recipe, simmering on top of the stove for 20 to 30 minutes.

SERVES 4.

Spicy Hamburger with Onion

INGREDIENTS

½ lb/250 g lean ground beef	2 cloves garlic
2 Tbsp/30 mL quick cooking oatmeal	1 egg
1 fresh chili (or ½ tsp/2.5 mL cayenne pepper)	Salt & pepper
	½ green pepper, diced
3 anchovies, chopped	Flour
2 Tbsp/30 mL oil	

Mix all the ingredients together, except the flour and oil, in a food processor. Form into patties or sausages and dip in flour. In a medium frypan heat the oil over medium high and fry sausages until golden brown. Serve with slices of raw onion.

SERVES 2.

Heart-Shaped Hamburgers

Love on a shoestring.

INGREDIENTS

½ lb/250 g ground beef	1 small onion, finely chopped
1 clove garlic, chopped	1 chili pepper, chopped
1 Tbsp/15 mL quick cooking oatmeal	1 egg
1 tsp/5 mL thyme	⅓ cup/80 mL chopped parsley
Salt & pepper	2 Tbsp/30 mL oil
Cooked & mashed potatoes	

Mix all the above ingredients together, except the oil and potatoes, and form into heart-shaped patties. Heat the oil in a medium frypan over medium-high heat and brown the patties. Remove to a plate and pipe mashed potatoes around the edge. Garnish with parsley.

SERVES 2.

Choucroute Garnie

(**shoe**-krute gar-**nee**)

Make sure you get top-quality sauerkraut—it makes all the difference in the world.

INGREDIENTS

- 4–5 slices bacon, chopped
- 1 apple, chopped
- Black pepper
- 2 cups/500 mL sauerkraut,
   rinsed & drained

- 1 onion, chopped
- 3–4 cloves garlic, chopped
- 1–2 tsp/5–10 mL caraway seeds
- 1 glass wine or beer
- 6–8 beef wieners

Fry the bacon in a large frypan over high heat. Stir in the onions and apple and cook until browned.

Turn down the heat, add the garlic, pepper, caraway seeds and sauerkraut and mix well together. Pour in the wine or beer and top with the wieners. Cover and simmer for 10 minutes or until piping hot.

Serve on top of mashed potatoes or with a nice loaf of pumpernickel bread.

SERVES 4.

Eggs

Eggs just don't have the dignity they once did. The first food, the simplest food, the riddle of life, a magnificent engineering job—the egg has a lot of magic going for it on a lot of counts, and it used to be the ultimate symbol of comfort. Wandering nomads couldn't keep chickens, but once they settled down, got a house, a well and something planted in the garden, they soon got hens, and of course they also got eggs. ■ Eggs meant luxury. People quickly learned that an egg in the bread dough made it rich, two eggs made it even richer, and three eggs turned it into cake. Suddenly cooking had class.

All the muffins we eat today, the angel food cakes, the Zabaglione in fancy restaurants, the mayonnaise, the Hollandaise, the Eggs Benedict—they're all *rich* things, things we remember with the specially satisfied pleasure that comes from something lasting lingering on the tongue. ■ That's the ultimate luxury—comfort. When I was a small boy, my allowance came from the chickens that preferred to lay their eggs in the garden, rather than the henhouse. We lived in the country, in a damp and chilly house, and almost every day in winter we sniffed and coughed and our noses ran. There was

no heat in the house, except for a small fireplace in the kitchen, and for a lot of years (any time is a long time when you're eight years old) I crawled into bed in my clothes, my socks, pants, shirt and sweater, and slowly, as the bed warmed up, I took them off, and kept them with me all night until one by one it was time to put them on again, get out of bed, and draw, with my finger, rude words in the frost on the inside of my window. ■ When it got too bad, a nose like a running tap and a face like a Christmas reindeer, my mother would decide that school was off for the day. Tomorrow I would take a note, but today I would spend in bed. "Nice and comfortable," she would say, and for that day only I would have a hot water bottle. In actual fact it was a brick, warmed in the oven and wrapped in two towels, and for perhaps half an hour it did help—it gave a little comfort and a little warmth. Most of the day I lay stiff as a plank and cold as a fish, my chest rubbed with goose grease mixed with camphorated oil, and I thought seriously (and as I remember with some anticipation) of death. I hoped God would forget all the good things I'd done and remember only the bad, so that he would be sure to send me to Hell, where at least it was warm. ■ But three times a day, on those long days in bed, real comfort arrived. My mother, by no means the best cook, could boil an egg to perfection, not soft but not hard, and with it she would bring me toast cut into finger-wide strips. She cut the top off the egg, and sat there, looking as happy as if she herself had laid it, while I dipped the toast into the egg and sucked it—rich and golden and warm and every mouthful telling me that life and love went on for ever and that tomorrow, just because of the magic of the egg, I would be better. ■

Herb Omelette

Fenugreek has a strong, bitter taste which is quite nice and interesting in small quantities—so restraint is the key in this dish.

INGREDIENTS

2 tsp/10 mL flour

3 eggs

Handful fresh parsley

2 small leeks (or small bunch chives)

½ tsp/2.5 mL fenugreek*

1 tsp/5 mL butter

1 tsp/5 mL baking powder

½ tsp/2.5 mL salt

Handful fresh cilantro

3 lettuce leaves

1 tsp/5 mL olive oil

Mix the flour and baking powder together in one bowl and whisk the eggs and salt together in another bowl. Beat the eggs into the flour and baking powder.

Chop the herbs, leeks and lettuce leaves and add them to the egg mixture along with the fenugreek.

Heat the oil and butter in a frypan over medium heat and pour in the mixture. Cover, lower the heat and cook for 5 minutes or until risen. Slide out onto a platter and serve immediately.

*Available at Indian or Oriental markets.   SERVES 2.

Eggs in Beer

If there's green eggs 'n ham let there be eggs 'n beer!

INGREDIENTS

1 bottle beer or ale

1 egg

Paprika

Pinch salt

1 slice toast

Chopped parsley

In a medium saucepan, heat the beer and salt until simmering and stir into a whirlpool. Break the egg into a saucer and gently tip into the liquid. Poach for 2 to 3 minutes. Remove the egg with a perforated ladle and serve on toast. Sprinkle with paprika and chopped parsley.

SERVES 1.

Indian Coconut Curry

This is a mild and slightly sweet curry—and a very economical dish to make.

INGREDIENTS

Few saffron threads
½ onion, grated
1 tsp/5 mL ground coriander
1 cup/250 mL grated coconut
Juice of ½ lime or lemon
3 hard-boiled eggs, halved
Cooked basmati rice

1 Tbsp/15 mL butter
½ onion, thinly sliced
½ tsp/2.5 mL paprika
½ tsp/2.5 mL salt
½ can (14 oz/398 mL) coconut milk
Chopped cilantro

Soak the saffron in 1 Tbsp/15 mL coconut milk for a few minutes.

Melt the butter in a medium-sized saucepan or frypan and sauté the onions, coriander and paprika. Add the grated coconut and stir well until it starts to brown. Add the salt, lime juice, coconut milk and saffron and stir until it thickens (don't boil). Simmer for 5 minutes and pour over the cooked eggs.

Serve with chopped cilantro and basmati rice.

SERVES 2.

Artichokes Plain & Simple *(see recipe on page 132)*

Oven-Baked Vegetables with Cornmeal Crust *(see recipe on page 129)*

Dandelion & Spinach Salad *(see recipe on page 146)* **and Fresh Strawberry Vegetable Salad** *(see recipe on page 150)*

Cold Tossed Noodles *(see recipe on page 117)*

Caviar (or Lumpfish Roe) Omelettes

If you're really picky get caviar but the truth is lumpfish tastes almost the same . . . and it's not quite so harsh on the wallet!

INGREDIENTS

- 3 eggs, beaten
- Salt & pepper
- 1 tsp/5 mL butter
- 1 jar red lumpfish roe
- Lemon wedges
- ½ eggshell water
- 1 tsp/5 mL thyme, and/or any herb of your choice
- 1 jar black lumpfish roe
- Sour cream
- Black pepper

Beat the eggs, water, salt, pepper and thyme together in a bowl.

Melt the butter in a small frypan over medium heat and tip in a quarter of the egg mixture. When the omelette has set, slide onto a plate and repeat with three more omelettes.

Allow them to cool and then roll them up lengthwise. Slice each one into about three pieces, sit them upright and top each slice with caviar and sour cream. Serve with lemon wedges and sprinkled with black pepper.

MAKES 9 HORS D'OEUVRES.

Coddled Eggs

You might want to cuddle after this one!

INGREDIENTS

- 1 tsp/5 mL butter
- 1 egg
- 1 Tbsp/15 mL cream
- Salt & pepper

Put the butter in an egg coddler or empty baby food jar. Break the egg into a saucer and tip into the jar. Top with the cream and seasoning, put the lid on and place in a saucepan of boiling water for 6 to 8 minutes or until the yolk has set.

SERVES 1.

> Probably one of the most private things in the world is an egg until it is broken. — **MFK Fisher**

Lettuce & Egg Gratin

INGREDIENTS

    1 Tbsp/15 mL butter   1 small lettuce, shredded

    Salt & pepper   ½ tsp/2.5 mL dill

    ¼ cup/60 mL 1% cottage cheese   ¼ cup/60 mL 1% yoghurt

    4 hard-boiled eggs, sliced   ½ cup/125 mL breadcrumbs

Preheat oven to 400°F/200°C.

Melt the butter and sauté the lettuce until wilted. Sprinkle with salt, pepper and dill. Blend the cottage cheese and yoghurt together and stir into the lettuce.

Pour into a small baking dish, add the sliced eggs and top with the breadcrumbs and a little more butter. Bake for 10 to 15 minutes or until brown and bubbling.

SERVES 2.

Cool Omelettes

Put your shades on for this one.

    4 eggs   1 Tbsp/15 mL tomato paste

    1 tsp/5 mL turmeric   Water

    Salt & pepper   2 Tbsp/30 mL butter

    Spinach leaves, washed & dried   Croutons

    Chopped parsley   Black olives

    2 hard-boiled eggs, sliced

Break 2 eggs into a bowl and beat with the tomato paste and a little water. Break the other 2 eggs into another bowl and beat with the turmeric and a little water. Season both with salt and pepper.

Melt 1 Tbsp butter in a frypan over medium-high heat and cook the tomato omelette. Remove and cool. Melt the remaining butter and cook the other omelette and cool.

Cut them both into strips and arrange them decoratively on a bed of spinach leaves. Garnish with croutons, chopped parsley, black olives and slices of hard-boiled eggs.

SERVES 2.

Beans &
Grainy Things

There is nothing cheaper than beans. Beans in a can if you must, but best of all plain simple dried beans, the basic comfort food of just about every culture's winter. White beans, fava beans, black beans, kidney beans, red beans, flageolets, fagioli, feves, call them what you will they're all beans, and they all respond to the same basic recipes, which take very little work and will cook slowly and aromatically while you do something else, or nothing. Beans are almost foolproof, and with meat, without meat, with fish, with root vegetables, even with rice, they finish up tasting good and comforting—nothing fancy, just a good plain cuddle. ■ Despite all these virtues, beans have a sad reputation in North American gastronomy. They're too cheap for the gourmets, too easy, they need no special pots, tools or classes and if that isn't enough there's the social consequences—the first commandment of polite society dinner parties still seems to be "Thou shalt not fart." ■ But beans are coming into their own. French bistro food is the next wave of gourmet fashion, and real bistro food means good simple food made in the morning to be served and eaten all day—the sort of food that goes well with a glass of house plonk, and is made using recipes handed down from a 70-year-old French grandma who killed and preserved her own pigs and ducks on the first day of last winter. ■ There are, however, easier alternatives, which will deliver for you, after two hours (most of which is sitting and inhaling the smells coming out of the kitchen) a glorious winter's supper with much the same character and flavour as a French cassoulet. Less meat, much less work, but you can still sit four or five around a table, lean on your elbows, eat with a fork, talk with your mouth full and, let's face it, fart. Like good friends. ■ All it needs is the courage to go out and buy a pound of dried beans. White beans are 90 cents a pounds, and Borlotto Lingua di Fuoco (Tongues of Fire, a lovely red and tan striped bean grown in Idaho) are $4.95. Your choice—they will all look much the same in the final dish, but some have more flavour. ■ So—it's five o'clock on a Saturday, and your friends are coming at seven. You haven't time for soaking beans overnight, so forget it. Just put the beans in a big saucepan, cover with boiling water by 2 inches, put the lid on and leave them for an hour. Drain them, cover with fresh water, add a bay leaf, bring to the boil (no salt, it makes them tough) and simmer, with the lid on, for 20 minutes. ■ Meanwhile, coarsely chop 1 large or 2 medium onions. Chop fine together 4 cloves of garlic and half a bunch of parsley. Slice a fairly thick pound or so of sausage (garlic sausage, kranske, chorizo, Italian, even good quality smokies), and check the beans for doneness. (They should be just a little firm, about 90 percent done.) Drain off the water, and keep it. ■ Fry the sausage slices in a spoonful of oil over medium heat until the fat starts to show and the outsides are slightly coloured. Add them to the beans, then fry the onions over medium heat until soft. Stir in the garlic and parsley, cook for two minutes more, then add 1 Tbsp ground cumin or 1 Tbsp cumin seeds, with 1 tsp oregano, 1 tsp ground pepper and 1 tsp salt and cook for a minute. Add a can of tomatoes, complete with their liquid, to the frypan, bring to the boil and stir it all into the beans, with a glass of red wine. ■ Bring the bean pot back to a slow simmer, stir in a teaspoon of cinnamon, and cook for an hour or so, stirring occasionally, particularly in the corners of the pot. If it looks too dry, add bean water or more red wine. If it looks a little thin, add 2 or 3 Tbsp of tomato paste. If you like it rich and funky, add 3 anchovy fillets, which will dissolve into the sauce. If you want a more exotic taste, add the zest (the outside coloured skin, not the white pith) of an orange. If you want chunks of ham in it, or duck breasts, or bits of lamb, fry them first, then add them, but it's just fine simply prepared with whatever sausage you can find. Just remember this is a peasant meal, not necessarily a balanced meal, so keep your vegetables for a salad. ■

Risotto Milanese

(ri-**zo**-toe mil-a-**nees**)

Cheap, easy, good old-fashioned peasant food that takes about half an hour to prepare. The Italians eat risotto by piling it into a mound on the plate and eating it from around the edges so ensuring that the middle stays hot.

INGREDIENTS

Few saffron threads

1 Tbsp/15 mL butter

½ onion, finely chopped

½ lb/250 g mushrooms, sliced

½ cup/125 mL Parmesan cheese, grated

2½ cups/625 mL chicken stock

1 Tbsp/15 mL olive oil

1 cup/250 mL arborio rice (or short-grain rice)

½ cup/125 mL dry white wine or sherry

Soak the saffron in a little hot stock for 5 minutes.

Melt the butter and oil in a large frypan and sauté the onion until it changes colour. Add the rice and saffron, stirring well to coat each grain. Over medium-low heat and stirring constantly, add the stock, a small amount at a time, until each amount is almost absorbed. If you freeze your stock in ice-cube trays, put in an ice cube at a time.

Add the mushrooms and wine and keep stirring; the rice should be tender but not soggy. If the rice is still hard, add more stock.

Add the Parmesan cheese and serve immediately with chopped parsley.

SERVES 2.

Broccoli Risotto

Another variation on this wonderful comfort food.

INGREDIENTS

1 cup/250 mL broccoli florets

½ cup/125 mL finely chopped broccoli

Cook the risotto as above, omitting the saffron and mushrooms, and substituting broccoli.

SERVES 2 AS A MAIN COURSE.

> **To keep a recipe book or card clean while cooking, place it under an upside-down glass pie plate. The curved bottom also magnifies the print.**

Polenta Mamaglia

(ma-**ma**-lee-ah)

Polenta is one of my favourite foods on a cold winter day.

INGREDIENTS

3 cups water	½ tsp/2.5 mL salt
1 cup/250 mL yellow cornmeal	2 Tbsp/30 mL butter

Boil the water and salt in large saucepan. Add the cornmeal in a steady stream, stirring all the time. Cook over a low heat for 15 to 20 minutes, stirring to avoid lumps. Pour onto a large platter, shape into a mound and pour melted butter over the top.

Garnish with any or all of the following:

Grilled fennel	Grilled green onions
Feta cheese	Hard-boiled eggs
Black olives	Roasted red peppers
Pickles	Fresh herbs

SERVES 4.

Grilled Polenta

A great way to deal with leftover polenta!

Make the polenta as above and pour into a shallow dish or baking sheet to about ½ in/1cm thickness. Cover and chill for an hour or overnight. Cut into slices, brush with olive oil and grill or fry until golden brown. Serve instead of pasta or rice.

SERVES 4.

Polenta Quattro Formaggio

(poh-**len**-ta **kwat**-tro for-**maj**-ee-o)

Polenta with four cheeses. *(See illustration facing page 65.)*

INGREDIENTS

1 Tbsp/15 mL butter	1 Tbsp/15 mL flour
Pepper	½–¾ cup/125–175 mL milk
2 Tbsp/30 mL cheddar cheese, grated	2 Tbsp/30 mL Gorgonzola cheese, cubed
2 Tbsp/30 mL mozzarella cheese, cubed	2 Tbsp/30 mL Parmesan cheese, grated
2 cups/500 mL cubed polenta	

Preheat oven to 375°F/190°C.

Make the polenta as above (see Polenta Mamaglia), then pour into a shallow dish or baking sheet to about ½ in/1cm thickness. Cover and chill for one hour or overnight, then cut into cubes. Set aside.

Melt the butter and stir in the flour to make a roux. Season with pepper and pour in the milk slowly to make a sauce. Add the cheeses and stir until smooth. Add the cubed polenta, pour into a baking dish and bake for 20 minutes or until the top is golden and bubbling.

SERVES 4.

Frijoles Negros

(free-**hole**-ays **nay**-gross)

It's good, healthy practice to have some meatless dishes in your repertoire, like this black beans and rice dish. You may be a little bit sceptical about this one but Frijoles Negros is surprisingly tasty and soothing. *(See illustration on overleaf facing page 65.)*

INGREDIENTS

2 Tbsp/30 mL olive oil
6 cloves garlic, whole
½ lb/250 g black beans, soaked &
    cooked for 1 hour, or
    1 can black beans
Bay leaf
Cooked white rice
2 bananas

1 white onion, finely chopped
Black pepper
Grated coconut
1 whole red, hot pepper
Salt
½ glass white wine
Handful chopped cilantro

Heat the oil in a frypan over medium heat and sauté the onion, whole garlic and black pepper. Add the beans, 1 Tbsp/15 mL grated coconut, red pepper, salt, bay leaf and white wine and cook until creamy.

Pour on top of the hot, white rice and garnish with chopped cilantro. Serve with side dishes of sliced bananas and grated coconut.

SERVES 4.

> **Rice remains the staple food for more than half of the world's population.**

Baked Tofu

Try some different soy sauces with this—regular, tamari and low-sodium are all easy to find.

INGREDIENTS

1 lb/500 g pressed tofu

4 Tbsp/60 mL soy sauce

2 Tbsp/30 mL sesame oil

2 Tbsp/30 mL sesame seeds

SAUCE

½ onion, finely chopped

1 Tbsp/15 mL soy sauce

1 tsp/5 mL sesame oil

1 Tbsp/15 mL vinegar

1 Tbsp/15 mL honey

Preheat oven to 350°F/180°C.

Cube the tofu and arrange in a single layer in a baking dish. Pour the sesame oil and soy sauce on top and sprinkle with sesame seeds. Bake for 25 minutes.

Mix together all ingredients for sauce. Remove tofu from oven and toss with sauce. Serve hot or cold with stir-fried veggies, or toss in salads or soups.

SERVES 4.

Drunken Beans & Chorizo

Don't let the name fool you. You'll be fine . . .

INGREDIENTS

2 Tbsp/30 mL oil

2 chorizo sausages, sliced

4 jalapeño peppers, whole

1 onion, finely chopped

3 tomatoes, chopped

1 can (14 oz/398 mL) pinto
    beans, drained

Salt & pepper

1 bottle beer

Tortillas

1 cup/250 mL cilantro, chopped

Heat the oil on medium-high heat and fry the chorizo and peppers until brown. Add the onion and tomatoes. Stir in the beans, salt and pepper and pour in the beer. Simmer over low heat until thickened, about 15 minutes.

Serve with tortillas and chopped cilantro.

SERVES 2.

Yoghurt Nut Rice

Every once in a while I like to give my rice a bit of a kick. Here's one way.

INGREDIENTS

2 cups/500 mL cooked rice

4 cups/1 L yoghurt

¼ cup/50 mL cashews, stir-fried

¼ cup/50 mL raisins, soaked & drained

¼ cup/50 mL walnuts, chopped fine

2 green chilis, minced

1 cup/250 mL chopped coriander

1 tsp/5 mL sugar

Salt

Mix all the above ingredients together and chill.

DRESSING

1 Tbsp/15 mL oil

1 tsp/5 mL cumin seeds

6 curry leaves

Heat the oil and add the seeds and leaves. When the seeds brown and pop, sprinkle the dressing over the rice.

SERVES 4.

Curried Kidney Beans

I should really think of a better name for this—to trick you into trying this one.

INGREDIENTS

2 Tbsp/30 mL butter

½ onion, chopped

2 Tbsp/30 mL curry powder

1 can kidney beans, drained

2 cloves garlic, chopped

3 Tbsp/45 mL yoghurt or sour cream

Salt & pepper

½ tsp/2.5 mL thyme

Juice of ½ lemon

Green onions

Parsley

Melt the butter in a frypan and stir in the onions. Add the curry powder. Mix in the beans, garlic, yoghurt or sour cream, salt, pepper, thyme and lemon juice and simmer gently. Serve with chopped green onions and parsley.

SERVES 1 OR 2.

Falafel

A Lebanese treat.

INGREDIENTS

½ onion, chopped
1 can (28 oz/796 mL) chickpeas,
    drained
2 cloves garlic
3 Tbsp/45 mL flour
1 tsp/5 mL ground cumin
1 tsp/5 mL ground coriander
¼ tsp/1 mL cayenne pepper
½ tsp/2.5 mL turmeric
1 tsp/5 mL baking powder
1 egg
Salt & pepper
⅓ cup/80 mL chopped mint
2 green onions, chopped

In a food processor or blender mix all ingredients, making sure the mixture stays grainy, not mushy. Pour into a bowl and let sit for 1 hour.

Roll into small balls. Heat ¾ in/1.5 cm oil in deep fry pan and drop falafel into it, cooking until brown and crispy on all sides. Serve with pita bread, humous, tomatoes and cucumbers.

SERVES 3.

Noodles & Pasta

N ot so very long ago, and not so very far away, noodles came two ways—long and thin and covered in tomato sauce, or short and curly and baked in cheddar sauce. Those dishes (and a poor cousin of real pizza) were all there was to "eating Italian." ■ We now eat noodles in hundreds of shapes and textures. Noodles with eggs, noodles without, rice-shaped noodles, long squiggly noodles, noodles from Asia, noodles from South America, fresh noodles, dry noodles, big fat heavy noodles, and noodles as light as air. Everybody has a favourite, and it doesn't really matter which shape you buy, although texture can sometimes make a difference. ■ Good recipes don't insist on exactly *this* or exactly *that*, and recipes which insist that nothing else will do were

probably written by nuclear physicists and will do nothing rewarding for your digestion. ■ Most pasta shapes are invented with certain uses in mind. If you're making a big, heavy sauce you might want a big, heavy pasta that won't suffocate underneath it. Likewise, a delicate little soup might turn tail and run at the sight of the larger noodles bearing down upon it. Other than that, go ahead and play. If you like angel hair better than penne, just do it. Pasta is pasta, and in your kitchen it's your show. ■ Making

your own pasta is a wonderful option. Ten minutes and you're somebody's Italian grandmother. 1 1/2 cups flour, 2 eggs, a little salt, a tablespoon of water—whizz it in the food processor until it forms a ball, then roll it out in sheets for the lightest, most wonderful lasagne in the world. You don't even have to boil it. Cut your sheets into strips and you've got fettucine. Not better than dry, just different. ■ But noodles don't end with pasta. All cultures use noodles in some form or other and ingredients depend on whatever grows best in whatever country they come from. Wheat is common, but any grain that can be ground is fair game for the noodle-makers. Textures change with ingredients, and for this reason it's probably a good idea to start with the kind of noodles recommended by the recipe, but if you can't find it—relax. Find yourself a good grocer who knows something about the food you're cooking, and let her suggest a substitute. ■ The most important thing to do with noodles is enjoy them. Someone once said "the Italians write poetry with pasta." Most importantly, noodles, any noodles, are easy to chew and digest and low in salt and fat. Soft, soothing, and a pleasure to eat. Kids love them, athletes live on them, and they're only as fattening as the sauce. ■

Fettucine with Shitake Mushrooms & Whiskey

If you can't find any fancy mushrooms, but you have button mushrooms on hand, this is still well worth trying.

INGREDIENTS

1 Tbsp/15 mL olive oil

1 clove garlic, finely chopped

4 Tbsp/60 mL soy sauce

1 Tbsp/15 mL sesame oil

Fettucine

½ lb/250 g shitake or oyster mushrooms

Pepper to taste

Whiskey (to your taste)

¾ cup/175 mL cream

Heat the oil and sauté the mushrooms, garlic and pepper until soft. Add the soy sauce, stir, add the whiskey and flambé. Add the sesame oil and pour in the cream to make a sauce.

Cook the pasta meanwhile, drain and toss with the sauce.

SERVES 2.

Spaghetti Frittata

Perfect for leftovers.

INGREDIENTS

2 Tbsp/30 mL olive oil

2 eggs

½ cup/125 mL milk

⅓ cup/80 mL grated cheese

Fresh basil

1 onion, chopped

2 egg whites

2 cups/500 mL cooked spaghetti

Fresh parsley

Salt & pepper

Heat 1 Tbsp/15 mL oil in a frypan and sauté the onions until lightly browned.

Whisk the eggs, egg whites and milk in a bowl and stir in all the rest of the ingredients. Add the mixture to the onions and cook until the bottom is brown, about 5 minutes.

Put a plate over the top and flip the frittata over to cook the other side. Alternatively, slide under the broiler to brown the top.

SERVES 2.

> How do you keep spaghetti from sliding off your plate? Use tomato paste!

Low-Fat Lasagne

INGREDIENTS

Lasagne strips

½ lb/250 g lean ground beef

¼ cup/50 mL bulgur

3 cloves garlic, chopped

½ tsp/2.5 mL cayenne pepper

1 tsp/5 mL pepper

1 Tbsp/15 mL flour

Breadcrumbs

1 Tbsp/15 mL olive oil

½ onion, chopped

1 8 oz/250 mL can crushed tomatoes

1 tsp/5 mL oregano

Juice of ½ lemon

½ cup/125 mL yoghurt

1 cup/250 mL cottage cheese

1 Tbsp/15 mL grated mozzarella cheese

Preheat oven to 350°F/180°C.

Cook the pasta in boiling water for 8 to 10 minutes and drain.

Heat the oil in a frypan and fry the meat until brown. Drain any excess fat from the pan. Add the onions and cook until soft. Stir in the bulgur, tomatoes, garlic, oregano, cayenne, lemon juice and pepper and stir for 5 minutes.

Layer the lasagne strips and meat mixture in an ovenproof dish. Blend the yoghurt and flour and pour over the top. Spread the cottage cheese over all and sprinkle with breadcrumbs and grated mozzarella. Bake for 20 to 30 minutes.

SERVES 4.

Fettucine with Salsa Limone

Simple and elegant.

INGREDIENTS

Fettucine

¼ cup/50 mL ricotta

¼ tsp/1 mL chili flakes

Zest of a lemon

1 Tbsp/15 mL butter

¼ cup/50 mL yoghurt

Chopped chives or green onions

Salt & pepper

Melt the butter and stir in the ricotta and yoghurt. Add the rest of the ingredients and heat gently. Serve with the cooked pasta and sprinkle with chopped parsley.

SERVES 2.

Linguine with Potatoes Pesto

Good rib-sticking fare.

INGREDIENTS

3 potatoes, sliced   1 lb/500 g linguine

Cook the potatoes in boiling, salted water for 3 minutes. Add the linguine and cook for a further 3 to 4 minutes. Drain and toss with one of the pesto sauces below.

PESTO WITH BASIL

Extra pesto can be stored in the freezer. For easy use, freeze pesto in an ice-cube tray overnight. Break out of tray and store frozen cubes in a freezer bag.

INGREDIENTS

2 cloves garlic, chopped
½ cup/125 mL olive oil
2 cups/500 mL fresh basil, chopped
3 Tbsp/45 mL Parmesan cheese
4 tbsp/60 mL pine nuts, toasted
Salt & pepper

Process in blender or food processor.

PESTO WITH CILANTRO

This cilantro pesto is also good with Thai dishes.

INGREDIENTS

2 cups/500 mL cilantro
2 cloves garlic
½ cup/125 mL walnuts
½ cup/125 mL peanut oil
Salt & pepper

Process in blender or food processor.

SERVES 4.

Pork & Sesame Noodles

Ginger and sesame are two of my favourite flavours. For an extra sesame bang, throw a little sesame oil on the noodles at the end. Remember, a little goes a long way.

INGREDIENTS

2 Tbsp/30 mL oil
Small bunch garlic chives (or
    ordinary chives & 1 clove garlic)
1 tsp/5 mL dried chili flakes
1 tsp/5 mL sugar
1 packet egg noodles
Chopped cilantro or parsley

¾ lb/375 g pork tenderloin, sliced diagonally
1 onion, chopped
3 slices ginger
1 Tbsp/15 mL balsamic vinegar
Salt & pepper
1 Tbsp/15 mL sesame seeds, toasted

Heat the oil and sauté the pork until lightly browned. Keeping the heat high, add the onion, garlic chives, ginger and chili flakes and stir in the vinegar, sugar, salt and pepper.

Cook the noodles and toss with the pork mixture and toasted sesame seeds. Serve with chopped cilantro or parsley.

SERVES 2.

Cold Tossed Noodles

A nice variation from the usual pasta salad. *(See illustration facing page 97.)*

INGREDIENTS

*1 bunch asparagus, stringy ends
  removed & cut diagonally*
¼ cup/50 mL rice vinegar
1 clove garlic, chopped
6 green onions, chopped

1 packet buckwheat noodles
¼ cup/50 mL soy sauce
1 tsp/5 mL sugar
4 slices ginger, minced
Chopped mint leaves

Cook the asparagus in boiling, salted water for about 3 minutes and plunge immediately into cold water. Drain.

Cook the noodles and toss with the asparagus and the rest of the ingredients while still hot, reserving the mint leaves. Put in the fridge to chill and serve with chopped mint.

SERVES 2.

Quick Spaghetti

Don't let the simplicity fool you.

INGREDIENTS

4 Tbsp/60 mL olive oil
2 cloves garlic, chopped
1 Tbsp/15 mL black pepper

Handful chopped parsley
3 anchovies
½ lb/250 g spaghetti

Heat the oil in a frypan and toss in the parsley and garlic. Add the anchovies and stir until they melt. Sprinkle in freshly ground black pepper, toss with the cooked spaghetti and serve immediately with more chopped parsley.

SERVES 2.

Vegetables

The best dinners start early, preferably just before breakfast, and on a fall morning, when the day doesn't yet know the difference between the last of summer and the first of winter and you, in bed and thinking about it, can't decide whether to wear a sweater or shirt sleeves. ■ Fall is the best time of year, the ripe time, the time of harvest festivals, of corn gods, of the juiciest fruits and loudest, noisiest of colours on the vegetable stands. Tomatoes, big ones and little ones, yellow ones, red ones and green—they've all sucked up the sunshine and turned it into a paintbox. Corn is suddenly its goldenest, the zucchini all shiny and greener than green and the markets are busting out in primary colours—they're all kids' paintings and it's impossible to walk past any of them without thinking of dinner. ■ The peppers are the most spectacular. Strings of skinny little red ones, brighter and glossier than lipstick, and great piles of splashy yellow ones, just hours off the vine and shinier than new cars. They come in great truckloads of colour from the sun-warmed fields and there's no way that any self-respecting stomach can pass by without spontaneously getting hungry. ■ Pumpkins are just round the corner, turkeys and sweet potatoes, cranberries and family dinners, but they have the habit of turning into big, complicated productions, and certainly not the sort of dinner that two of you want to think about over a cappuccino. Coffee seems to be the best way to start this dinner, a cappuccino and a pain au chocolat. You will need a decent loaf, so you take that extra bit of trouble to get to your best bakery—the one closest to the farmer's market. You buy a *New York Times,* or the British *Financial Post* (a surprisingly interesting paper, largely and intelligently concerned with matters far beyond finance), sip on the caffeine, watch the people go by and ready yourself for dinner's selection. ■ Slowly and meditatively, past the broccoli, past the asparagus maybe a little too expensive, to the chanterelles also expensive but somehow an affordable luxury, so you buy half a pound. The corn may be better on the other side of the market so you wait (there is much expertise in the studying of corn, without stripping the husks off). There are tomatoes riper now than they will ever be again, there are fresh hazelnuts (freeze them unshelled in small bags and occasionally, in the middle of winter, take out a few for dessert, just to remind you of today), but most of all, on this walk, you should watch for the peppers. ■ You choose carefully, with an eye for symmetry, for shape and for shine, and you take home four, two red, two green, or one each of red, yellow, green and purple. You may need at this time to take another cappuccino, another look at the boats, and a bit more of the newspaper, but it will then be time for the best three tomatoes you can find, and a serious search for a bunch of firm and upright basil and finally an onion—not just any old onion, nothing ordi-

nary, but a perfect onion. This is your supper you are anticipating, this is your belly kicking tires, this is more important than choosing a shirt or a pair of shoes, and at least half the enjoyment comes in the foreplay, which you just can't rush. ■ You have a loaf of bread, and you may want to stop for an assortment of olives, although my stomach almost always insists on the little black oil-cured ones. A hundred grams or so of Kefalatiri cheese (Greek, white, an interesting blend of mild and tart) or, if you have the money, a small amount of chevre which, with a couple of ripe local pears, makes for a great dessert. That's the shopping done, apart from half a dozen free-range eggs and of course an assumption that at home you have some olive oil. ■ And finally you go home, to a bath, to the ball game, the dog or the cat, you spread your iridescent trophies all over the kitchen, you gloat awhile, and 20 minutes before you want to eat you start supper, a Piperade Basquaise. ■ Easy. 3 tablespoons of olive oil in a hot pan over high heat, and add the onion, peeled and chopped fine. Cook for 1 minute, while you dice the peppers. Add the peppers, still over high heat, and cook for 2 minutes, while you chop the tomatoes, making sure the juice doesn't all escape. Add the basil, cut in thin shreds, the tomatoes, the chanterelles, sliced, a teaspoon of ground black pepper and a pinch or two of salt. Cook for four minutes, stirring, and still over high heat, then dump in, all at once, 4 or 6 eggs, beaten lightly. Turn the heat to low (this stops the eggs becoming stringy) and stir gently and meditatively while the whole thing turns creamy, colourful and comforting. Take off the heat while it still looks a little liquid and underdone, and by the time you get sat down at the table the heat in the pan will have finished the cooking. ■ That's it. If you don't want to call it a Piperade Basquaise, then call it a Chachouka. Or even a Denver Omelette. ■

Carrot & Nut Mélange

Tarragon brings a lovely sweet and fragrant quality to this dish.

INGREDIENTS

2 carrots

1 Tbsp/15 mL butter

Chopped mixed nuts

Salt & pepper

1 Tbsp/15 mL oil

Chopped almonds

1 tsp/5 mL tarragon

Cut the carrots into matchsticks. Heat the oil and butter and fry the carrots, nuts, tarragon, salt and pepper over medium heat until golden. Decorate with parsley.

SERVES 2.

Cipolle e Piselli in Umido   (chi-**pole**-ay ay pi-**sell**-ee in oo-**mee**-doe)

Braised peas and onions sound so mundane. But give the dish an Italian name and the transformation is amazing.

INGREDIENTS

2 Tbsp/30 mL olive oil

½ lb/250 g small pickling
    onions, peeled & blanched

½ cup/125 mL chicken stock

Yoghurt or cream

1 clove garlic, chopped

2 Tbsp/30 mL parsley, chopped

1 packet frozen peas

Salt & pepper

Heat the oil and sauté the garlic and parsley. Add the onions, peas and stock. Cover and simmer for 8 minutes. Add salt and pepper and stir in the yoghurt or cream.

SERVES 2.

Squashed Potatoes

Kids love this one.

INGREDIENTS

1 lb/500 g leftover new potatoes,
    boiled or roasted

1–2 Tbsp/15–30 mL olive oil

Chopped parsley

Crush each potato by holding in your hands (use a towel if necessary) and pressing down firmly. Brush the tops of the potatoes with oil and broil until brown and crispy, about 5 to 8 minutes. Serve with Carrot Sauce topped with parsley.

CARROT SAUCE

1½ lb/750 g leftover cooked carrots	1 glass (6 oz/175 mL) white wine
1 Tbsp/15 mL butter	1½ Tbsp/22 mL flour
1 tsp/5 mL mustard	¼ tsp/1 mL cinnamon
¼ tsp/1 mL nutmeg	Fresh mint
Salt & pepper	

Blend the carrots in a food processor or blender, diluting with a glass of white wine.

In a saucepan over medium-low heat melt the butter and add the flour to make a roux. Slowly add the carrot purée and the rest of the ingredients until thick and creamy.

SERVES 4.

Asparagus with Yoghurt

A thick stalk of asparagus is just as good as a pencil-thin one, if it's not woody.

INGREDIENTS

1 lb/500 g asparagus

Boil or lightly steam the asparagus with a little water and a pinch of salt for 3 to 4 minutes (or just until the colour brightens). Plunge immediately into cold water to stop the cooking process and drain. Serve with:

*½ cup/125 mL mayonnaise or
    Tofu Dressing (see below)*
½ cup/125 mL yoghurt
1 tsp/5 mL dill
Pinch cayenne pepper

Blend all the above ingredients and pour over the asparagus.

SERVES 4 (unless you really like asparagus, in which case it serves 2.)

Asparagus with Tofu Dressing

A little sweet, a little sour.

INGREDIENTS
   1 lb/500 g asparagus

Boil or lightly steam asparagus for 3 to 4 minutes (or just until the colour brightens). Plunge immediately in cold water to stop the cooking process and drain.

TOFU DRESSING
1 block firm tofu	*1 tsp/5 mL maple syrup*
½ tsp/2.5 mL salt	*¼ cup/50 mL oil*
¼ cup/50 mL vinegar or lemon juice	*1 clove garlic*

Blend all the above ingredients together, adding a little water if necessary, and serve with asparagus.

SERVES 4.

Grilled Leeks

This is perfect for the toaster oven.

INGREDIENTS
   6 leeks
   1 Tbsp/15 mL sesame oil
   Pinch cayenne pepper
   2 Tbsp/30 mL soy sauce

Cut leeks into finger lengths and brush with sesame oil. Broil until they turn brown. Mix the cayenne pepper and soy sauce together and brush over the leeks.

Return to broiler and cook for about 10 minutes until tender.

SERVES 2.

> The ancient Greek word for carrot, *philon*, comes from the Greek word for love, as this root was considered an aphrodisiac.

Carrot Kimpura

Don't be daunted at the thought of preparing Japanese food. Because of the traditional scarcity of fuel, Japanese food for the most part requires only fast cooking. It's the best fast food around.

INGREDIENTS

3 carrots
½ tsp/2.5 mL salt
3 hot red chili peppers
1 Tbsp/15 mL mirin*
   (or 1 Tbsp/15 mL white
   wine + 1 tsp/5 mL sugar)
1 Tbsp/15 mL toasted sesame seeds

2 Tbsp/30 mL vinegar
Pepper to taste
2 Tbsp/30 mL olive oil
1 Tbsp/15 mL sake* (or whiskey)
1 Tbsp/15 mL sugar
3 Tbsp/45 mL soy sauce

Cut the carrots into matchsticks and soak in vinegar, salt and pepper for 10 minutes. Remove and dry.

Heat the chili peppers in a dry frypan over high heat until they start to smoke. Add the carrots and oil and stir well. Pour in the mirin, sake, sugar and soy sauce and boil until the carrots are glazed.

Tip onto a plate and sprinkle with toasted sesame seeds. Good hot or cold.

*Available in Japanese markets or specialty liquor stores.   SERVES 2.

Carrots & Honey in Vodka

These have a nice bite to them.

INGREDIENTS

1 Tbsp/15 mL olive oil or butter
Zest & juice of an orange
1 Tbsp/15 mL honey

3 or 4 carrots, sliced into rounds
Few drops tabasco
3 Tbsp/45 mL vodka

Heat the oil over high heat and stir in the carrots. Add the orange juice and zest, tabasco, honey and vodka and boil for 1 to 2 minutes.

SERVES 2.

Lebanese Cumin Carrots

If you don't know about cumin, then I suggest you give it a try. It's available in just about any supermarket. Very distinctive, very special.

INGREDIENTS

2 cups/500 mL cooked, mashed carrots
1 Tbsp/15 mL wine vinegar
1 tsp/5 mL paprika
1 tsp/5 mL ground cumin
Salt & pepper
Cilantro

3 Tbsp/45 mL olive oil
2 cloves garlic
1 tsp/5 mL chili powder
2 Tbsp/30 mL cumin seeds, toasted
Black olives

Mix together all the ingredients, saving the black olives, cilantro and 1 Tbsp/15 mL toasted cumin seeds as a garnish. Blend in a food processor or blender until a thick purée, pour onto a dish and scatter with chopped olives, cilantro and cumin seeds.

SERVES 2.

Yoghurt & Spinach

Substitute the turmeric for lots of dill. Either way, this is a great dish to throw together in a hurry. Frozen spinach is just as good as the fresh—and you don't have to wash it.

INGREDIENTS

1 Tbsp/15 mL oil
1 or 2 onions, finely sliced
2 lb/1 kg fresh spinach or
    1 packet frozen spinach
½ tsp/2.5 mL turmeric
Salt & pepper
1 cup/250 mL yoghurt

Heat the oil and sauté the onions until browned. Stir in the spinach, turmeric, salt and pepper. Cover and cook 5 minutes or until the spinach is soft. Drain and cool.

Stir in the yoghurt. Serve as a side dish or on its own.

SERVES 4.

> **Spinach is the broom of the stomach.—French proverb**

(l. to r.) **Flower Herb Vinegar, Mango Chutney and Prik Dong** *(see recipes on pages 156–7)*

Flower Pot Bread *(see recipe on page 162)*

Raspberry Vodka *(see recipe on page 188)*

No-Bake Chocolate Cake *(see recipe on page 174)* **and Chocolate-Dipped Grapes** *(see recipe on page 179)*

Oven-Baked Vegetables with Cornmeal Crust

Feel free to substitute vegetables. Use what's in season and throw in a bit of thyme, or basil, or rosemary, or why not oregano. Use your imagination. *(See illustration facing page 96.)*

INGREDIENTS

8 small, new potatoes, halved

1 green pepper, sliced

1 red onion, quartered

4 asparagus spears, chopped

Salt & pepper

1 red pepper, sliced

3 roma tomatoes, quartered

1 small eggplant, chopped

4 Tbsp/60 mL olive oil

Preheat oven to 425°F/220°C.

Pack the vegetables into a baking dish, not too tightly or they will turn soggy. Add the oil, salt and pepper and toss well.

Bake in oven for 10 minutes, turning the vegetables occasionally, then pour the Cornmeal Crust over top and bake for a further 10 minutes.

CORNMEAL CRUST

⅔ cup/160 mL flour

½ tsp/2.5 mL salt

2 eggs

¼ cup/50 mL warm water

½ cup/125 mL cornmeal

2 tsp/10 mL baking powder

¼ cup/50 mL milk

2 Tbsp/30 mL olive oil

Sift the flour, cornmeal, salt and baking powder. Beat the eggs, milk, water and oil and blend into the flour mixture. Pour over the vegetables and bake as described above.

SERVES 4 TO 6.

Sweet & Sour Cabbage

A great tasty side dish for those watching their waistlines.

INGREDIENTS

2 Tbsp/30 mL olive oil

½ green cabbage, cored & shredded

1 can (13 oz/370 mL) chopped tomatoes

1 Tbsp/15 mL honey

½ tsp/2.5 mL salt

1 onion, chopped

1 tsp/5 mL pepper

2 Tbsp/30 mL capers (optional)

1 Tbsp/15 mL vinegar

Preheat oven to 375°F/190°C.

Heat the oil in a frypan and sauté the onion until softened. Add the cabbage and black pepper and stir until well coated. Add the tomatoes, capers, honey, vinegar and salt, stir well and pour into a baking dish. Bake for 20 minutes until bubbling.

SERVES 4.

Rolled Cabbage & Spinach

The pale and dark green contrast of these rolls is very pretty next to a piece of chicken or fish. Throw a sliced tomato or some roasted red pepper on the plate and you have created a veritable work of art.

INGREDIENTS

1 packet frozen spinach or

½ lb/250 g fresh spinach

1 Chinese cabbage

1 Tbsp/15 mL soy sauce

Cook the spinach according to package directions or, if fresh, in a small amount of water until just wilted. Remove and drain well, squeezing out any excess water.

Blanch the cabbage leaves and drain. Lay out 2 or 3 leaves to make a square and arrange some of the spinach in tight rolls across. Roll up into a tight cylinder and squeeze out any extra water.

Leave for 10 minutes and slice diagonally. Serve warm with soy sauce.

SERVES 4.

Red Cabbage Kimchi

If you haven't tried balsamic vinegar, treat yourself to a small bottle. Unscrew the cap and take a good deep whiff. You'll never look back. Not only does it make its indelible mark on this very tasty dish, but it really is spectacular in a simple vinaigrette over some hearty greens.

INGREDIENTS

1 Tbsp/15 mL olive oil
6 slices fresh ginger, chopped
3 hot red chili peppers
1 cup/250 mL red wine
2 Tbsp/30 mL brown sugar
1 Tbsp/15 mL butter

½ red onion, chopped
3 cloves garlic, whole
½ red cabbage, shredded
2 Tbsp/30 mL balsamic vinegar
Salt & pepper

Heat the oil in a saucepan and fry the onion. Sprinkle in black pepper and add the ginger, garlic and chili peppers. Stir in the cabbage and cook for 5 minutes or until softened. Add the wine, vinegar, sugar and salt and simmer for a further few minutes.

Stir in the butter at the last minute and serve hot or cold.

SERVES 4.

Asparagus Parmesan

Asparagus is such an elegant vegetable—and it's considered polite to eat it with your fingers!

INGREDIENTS

2 Tbsp/30 mL ground almonds
Salt & pepper
½ lb/250 g asparagus,
   stringy ends removed
Juice of ½ orange

1 Tbsp/15 mL Parmesan cheese
1 Tbsp/15 mL olive oil or butter
1 Tbsp/15 mL white wine
½ tsp/2.5 mL salt

Mix the ground almonds, Parmesan cheese, salt & pepper together. Heat the oil in a frypan over high heat and lay the asparagus in the pan. Pour in the wine, sprinkle with salt and cook for 2 to 3 minutes.

Remove to a plate and sprinkle with the almond mixture. Drizzle with orange juice and serve.

SERVES 2.

Sautéed Cherry Tomatoes

Simple and delicious. A nice complement to just about any plate.

INGREDIENTS

1 Tbsp/15 mL olive oil

1 onion, chopped

1 Tbsp/15 mL vinegar

Salt & pepper

1 cup/250 mL cherry tomatoes

1 Tbsp/15 mL oregano

1 tsp/5 mL sugar

Heat the olive oil in a frypan and tip in the cherry tomatoes. Add the chopped onion and cook until softened. Add the rest of the ingredients and stir for about 2 minutes. Serve hot.

SERVES 2.

Oh Baby Baby Artichokes

Whenever you find baby artichokes in the market, buy them. They're hard to find but so good.

INGREDIENTS

8–10 baby artichokes

6 cloves garlic, chopped

½ tsp/2.5 mL salt

2 Tbsp/30 mL olive oil

1 Tbsp/15 mL pepper

Juice of a lemon

Remove the outer leaves of the artichokes, trim the stalks and toss in lemon juice and water until ready to use. Heat the oil in a frypan, cut the artichokes in half and lay them, cut side down, in a single layer in the pan. Add the garlic and pepper, put the lid on and cook until the artichoke bottoms go brown.

Sprinkle with salt, squeeze the lemon juice over them and serve.

SERVES 2.

Artichokes Plain & Simple

Remove the outer leaves from large artichokes and poach in boiling, salted water for 35 minutes. Drain and serve.

Pull off the leaves, dip each one in a dish of olive oil or melted butter and suck the meat from the ends. When you reach the middle, remove all the whiskery parts and eat the heart—the prime part! *(See illustration on overleaf facing page 96.)*

"Pasta" & Goat Cheese

Spaghetti squash is really a fun discovery. I use it with just about any pasta sauce.

INGREDIENTS

1 spaghetti squash

1 Tbsp/15 mL olive oil

½ cup/125 mL chopped walnuts

½ cup/125 mL cream

2 Tbsp/30 mL Parmesan cheese

Salt & pepper

1 Tbsp/15 mL butter

4 cloves garlic, finely chopped

Handful chopped parsley

4 oz/125 g goat's cheese

Handful of chopped basil

Halve and cook the spaghetti squash in boiling water for 15 minutes or until tender. Drain and pull out the strands with a fork to make spaghetti.

Melt the butter and oil in a frypan and sauté the garlic, walnuts, parsley and pepper. Remove. Mix together the cream, goat's cheese and Parmesan cheese. Toss the spaghetti squash with the walnut and cheese mixtures, basil, salt and pepper. Serve hot.

SERVES 4.

Stuffed Roasted Onion

Onions are essential as the base for so many dishes and so we often forget about them as the main attraction. They're worthy of centre stage every now and again.

INGREDIENTS

1 onion

1 carrot, chopped

Bunch parsley

Salt & pepper

1 slice bacon, chopped

2 slices stale bread

1 tsp/5 mL thyme

1 Tbsp/15 mL oil

Preheat oven to 375°F/190°C.

Cut a slice off the top of the onion and scoop out most of the inside, leaving a thick outer shell. Peel the skin off and put into boiling water for just 2 minutes. Remove and drain.

Chop up the inside of the onion and fry with the bacon. Put the onion, bacon, carrot and bread into a food processor. Season with the parsley, thyme, salt, pepper and oil and blend.

Stuff this mixture into the middle of the onion and place in a greased baking dish. Bake in oven for 20 to 25 minutes.

SERVES 1.

Parsnip, Potato & Ginger Soufflé

Everyone seems to have forgotten about the joys of soufflé.

INGREDIENTS

2 cups/500 mL cooked, mashed parsnips

½ cup/125 mL milk or cream

1 tsp/5 mL black pepper

Zest of ½ lemon or orange

1 cup/250 mL cooked, mashed potato

3 Tbsp/45 mL butter

½ tsp/2.5 mL salt

2 tsp/10 mL grated fresh ginger

3 eggs

Beat together the parsnips and potatoes with the butter, milk, salt, pepper, ginger and lemon or orange zest until fluffy.

Separate the eggs and beat in the yolks. In a separate bowl whip the egg whites until stiff and fold into the parsnip mixture. Pour into a medium-sized greased soufflé dish and bake for 30 to 40 minutes.

SERVES 4.

Potato & Parsnip Latkes

Rich, tasty European fare. You don't have to be a grandmother to make these.

INGREDIENTS

1 potato, grated

1 parsnip, grated

1 egg

1 Tbsp/15 mL flour

1 tsp/5 mL grated ginger

Salt & pepper

1 Tbsp/15 mL oil

Mix together the potato, parsnip, egg, flour, ginger, salt and pepper in a bowl. Heat the oil in a frypan and drop in spoonfuls of the mixture. Pat down into little cakes and fry until lightly browned.

Drain and serve immediately with chopped green onion and sour cream.

SERVES 2.

Potatoes are almost 78 percent water, high in carbohydrates and contain 2 percent protein.

Peppers Stuffed with Corn, Potato, Egg & Violet Salad

Special dinner party fare.

INGREDIENTS

1 each of red, green, yellow &
  orange peppers
4 hard-boiled eggs, chopped
½ red pepper, finely diced
½ yellow pepper, finely diced
1 tsp/5 mL capers, finely chopped
½ tsp/2.5 mL curry powder
Fresh organic violets

2 fresh corn cobs, cooked
2 cups/500 mL diced new potatoes, cooked
2 sticks celery, finely chopped
½ green pepper, finely diced
½ onion, finely chopped
½ cup/125 mL mayonnaise
Salt & pepper
Watercress

Cut a slice off the top of each pepper and remove the seeds. Cut the sides to resemble flower petals and set aside.

Cut the kernels off the corn and mix with the rest of the ingredients, reserving the violets and watercress. Stuff the peppers with the mixture, garnish with violets and lay on a bed of watercress. Serve a different-coloured pepper for each person.

SERVES 4.

Fu Fu

Exotic mashed potatoes.

INGREDIENTS

2 yams
1 plantain (or green banana)
Juice of ½ lemon
Salt & pepper
Chopped parsley

Parsley—the jewel of herbs, both in the pot and on the plate.

Cook the yams in boiling water until tender, about 30 minutes. Drain, peel and mash them with the plantain, lemon juice, salt, pepper and chopped parsley.

SERVES 4.

Sweet Potatoes with Orange & Coconut

INGREDIENTS

2 sweet potatoes, cooked

2 Tbsp/30 mL sugar

2 Tbsp/30 mL grated coconut

1 orange, peeled & sliced

1 can coconut milk

1 Tbsp/15 mL butter

Preheat oven to 375°F/190°C.

Slice the sweet potatoes and layer in a greased baking dish with the orange slices. Mix the sugar, coconut milk and grated coconut and pour over the potatoes. Dot with butter and bake for 20 minutes.

SERVES 2.

Brunede Kartoffler

A fancy name for a simple dish. I often throw in a little extra dill.

INGREDIENTS

½ lb/250 g potatoes

1 tsp/5 mL salt

3 Tbsp/45 mL sugar

3 Tbsp/45 mL butter

1 Tbsp/15 mL chopped fresh dill

Cook the potatoes in boiling, salted water until just tender, about 10 to 15 minutes. Drain.

Lightly brown the sugar in a frypan, stirring constantly, and stir in the butter. Add the potatoes, shaking the pan to make sure they all get coated and glazed. Serve hot with chopped dill.

SERVES 2.

Anchovy Potatoes

Anchovies should be a staple in everyone's pantry.

INGREDIENTS

1 can anchovies

3 potatoes, cooked, peeled & cubed

1 tsp/5 mL rosemary, sage or thyme

2 cloves garlic, chopped

1 tsp/5 mL pepper

Chopped parsley

Melt the anchovies in a frypan and add the garlic and potatoes. Stir well until the potato cubes are brown, sprinkle with pepper and rosemary and serve with chopped parsley.

SERVES 2.

Stir Fry of Chinese Vegetables

INGREDIENTS

2 Tbsp/30 mL oil

5 slices ginger

½ cup/125 mL broccoli, chopped

2 Tbsp/30 mL dried mushrooms,
*   soaked for 10 minutes,*
*   drained & sliced*

1 tsp/5 mL sugar

2 Tbsp/30 mL soy sauce

1 tsp/5 mL cornstarch

1 onion, chopped

½ cup/125 mL carrots, diced

1 cup/250 mL bok choy, chopped

½ cup/125 mL bean sprouts

1 red pepper, diced

½ tsp/2.5 mL salt

1 glass stock

1 Tbsp/15 mL sesame oil

Heat the oil and stir in the onion, ginger, carrots and broccoli. Add the bok choy, mushrooms, bean sprouts and red peppers, stir-frying for about 2 minutes. Add the salt, sugar, stock, soy sauce and sesame oil.

Mix the cornstarch to a paste with a little water and stir into the vegetables to glaze. Serve immmediately.

SERVES 4 AS A SIDE DISH.

Steamed New Potatoes

Melt 2 Tbsp/30 mL butter, stir in ½ cup/125 mL of chopped fresh mint, ½ tsp/2.5 mL salt and ½ tsp/2.5 mL vinegar and pour over steamed new potatoes.

Baked Corn

Preheat oven to 500°F/250°C.

    Soak the corn, with husks on, in a bucket of water until you're ready to cook them. Bake for 10 to 12 minutes. Pull back the husks to make a natural handle and eat with butter, salt and pepper.

Refried Butter Beans

You either like them or you don't.

INGREDIENTS

    3 Tbsp/45 mL olive oil   *Juice of ½ lemon*
    1 packet (2 cups/500 mL approx.)   *Salt & pepper*
      frozen lima beans   *Chopped parsley*

Heat the olive oil in a frypan and fry the beans until golden brown, about 5 to 10 minutes. Sprinkle with lemon juice, salt and pepper and serve with chopped parsley.

SERVES 4.

Salads

In case you didn't know, getting thin was a $30 billion industry last year in the United States. It's a guilt industry, like the old-time religions: fat is sinful and sin itself is largely anything you can imagine. Women are pushovers for the weight-loss evangelists—70 percent of women with normal weights say they want to be thinner, but 23 percent of underweight women have the same ambition. While women are the main subscribers, men are not insignificant members of the congregation of guilt. According to last year's statistics, 50 percent of women in the United States are always on some kind of diet, and 30 percent of men.

■ "If he be not hungry, 'tis not fit he should eat," said John Locke, a doctrine by which he lived for a healthy 72 years, in a time when male life expectancy was 50. This doctrine of simple restraint may have been years ahead of its time. The seventeenth century had its share of tosspots, lardbellies, and flabberguts, but fat was more envied than pitied, more admired than despaired of, because fat meant rich, and nobody thought that a state to be remedied. Most of all, nobody felt guilty about it. But not any more. ■ A market opportunity like this, which takes in the old and the young, the rich and the poor, the dim and the bright, is altogether too good to miss, and there are more diet gurus than TV evangelists. Ninety-five percent of people who lose weight on crash diets put it all back (and more) within three years. More fat, more guilt, more diets—for the promoters it's better than the lotteries. They don't even have to give prizes and they quite literally live off the fat of the land. ■ All fad diets have one thing in common. They're all easy. You can lose weight as simply as you can become a matchbook brain surgeon. Six easy lessons, send money. There is a choice of guilt, greed or shame, but they all offer salvation—a size smaller, an improved love life, a better job. They all treat you like a patient, a candidate for a make-over, and they all offer insecurity as a permanent guest at your table: "Was it two teaspoonfuls three times or three teaspoons twice? Is one avocado before dinner the same as two eggs after, and it doesn't mention bacon so will that be okay?". ■ Food, in the hands of the diet evangelists, becomes as joyless as filling the gas tank, something to be counted, faked and finally feared. Food equals fat, they say, and we let them persuade us into sugar substitutes, artificial bacon, lite "beer" and fartless beans, all of which distance us from the realities and the

pleasures of our gastro-intestinal tract. Choice based on taste, on quality and even on the seasons gives way to calories, waistlines and, of all things in this land of plenty, diet supplements. We live in a country of abundance, a year-long harvest festival, but feasts have become occasions for regret: "Oh God, I'm not going to eat another thing until Thursday". ■ It's taking all the fun out of food. I went to a wedding last week and the bride, skinny as a bean pole, spent most of her time talking to people about her diet, and the changes she was going to make in her new husband's diet. And of

course his life. The food was awful—it was dull and tasteless and joyless, it was full of fibre and low-fat this and low-cal that, everybody left early and nobody had a good time. ■ But I went to another wedding a week before where the main ingredients were asparagus, yoghurt and wine. A vast pile of bright green asparagus, lightly cooked, a big bowl of yoghurt with fresh dill whipped into it, and that was basically it. Not traditional at all, but really fresh and really self-indulgent—there was more asparagus than you could dream of, and the guests loved it, it was something they could over-indulge in, and still drive home, full of a good time, sober and guilt-free. ■ If you really feel you have to lose a litle weight, there are lots of equally simple things you can do without worrying, and end up feeling good about it. The food magazines are full of references to the "Mediterranean Diet," which really means eating the way that a lot of people have done for years—the Italians, the Greeks, the Spaniards—all the people who live in sunny warm climates where olives grow and sheep are milked, where the hillsides grow grapes and the valleys produce lots of fruit and vegetables. They eat a lot less meat, olive oil instead of butter, lots of fresh fruit and vegetables—that's a common shopping list. But the real feature of their diet pleasure—they eat really fresh things, when they're in season, and they eat them with a passion close to gluttony. When the artichoke season is over the asparagus season starts, then the rapini season and then the radicchio, each one to be fully enjoyed and eaten until you can eat no more. ■ It's also good economics. Stuff in season is cheap. But nobody makes any money out of this kind of diet, there's no books to buy, no pills, no charts—all you do is walk round the market as often as you can and buy what's freshest and cheapest. . . . And if it's salad you're after, just go easy on the dressing. ■

Sauerkraut Salad

I bet you didn't think that sauerkraut could be so simple.

INGREDIENTS

½ cup/125 mL chopped walnuts

2 cups/500 mL sauerkraut,
    well rinsed & drained

1 red onion, thinly sliced

1 Tbsp/15 mL grated horseradish
    (fresh or from a bottle)

3 Tbsp/45 mL olive oil

1 apple, cored & diced

1 pear, cored & diced

Salt & pepper

1 red pepper, diced

Heat a medium-sized frypan and sauté the walnuts in 1 tsp/5 mL olive oil until lightly browned and smoky. Arrange the sauerkraut, apple, pear and red onion in a salad bowl. Mix together the remaining olive oil, horseradish, salt and pepper and toss with the salad. Scatter the sautéed walnuts and diced red pepper over the top and serve.

SERVES 4.

Beetroot & Feta Salad

INGREDIENTS

½ cup/125 mL chopped almonds

1 Tbsp/15 mL butter

1 can (14 oz /398 mL) beets,
    drained & cubed

1 cup/250 mL feta cheese, cubed

Pinch nutmeg

Pinch cinnamon

1 orange

2 Tbsp/30 mL chopped parsley

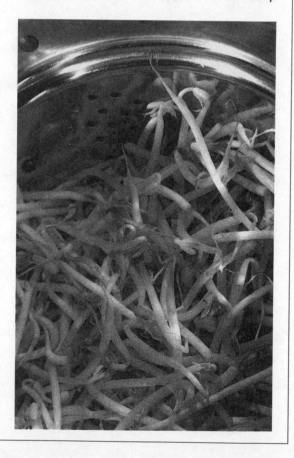

Heat a small frypan and melt the butter. Sauté the almonds until lightly browned and remove. Mix with beets, feta, nutmeg and cinnamon in a salad bowl or on a plate and serve garnished with orange slices and chopped parsley.

SERVES 2.

Cartwheel Salad

A nice appetizer for an elegant dinner party.

INGREDIENTS

4 oranges

Juice of ½ lemon

Chives

4 avocados

Salt & pepper

Peel and segment each orange. Halve, peel and slice each avocado. Arrange alternate orange and avocado slices in circles to produce a cartwheel effect. Drizzle with a little lemon juice and season with salt and pepper. Decorate with finely chopped chives.

SERVES 4.

Fresh Asparagus with Strawberry Vinaigrette

A colourful splash to start a special meal.

INGREDIENTS

2 bunches asparagus, stringy
  ends removed

3 Tbsp/45 mL olive oil

½ tsp/2.5 mL salt

½ lb/250 g strawberries

Zest of an orange

1 Tbsp/15 mL vinegar

1 tsp/5 mL pepper

Cover the bottom of a large frypan with water and bring to the boil. Add the asparagus, sprinkle with salt, cover and cook for 3 to 4 minutes. Remove the asparagus and plunge immediately into cold water and drain.

Blend the strawberries, orange zest, oil, vinegar, salt and pepper and drizzle over the asparagus.

SERVES 4.

> **Did you know that common store or button mushrooms have only 66 calories per pound?**

Dandelion & Spinach Salad

Pick the dandelions from your lawn (or your neighbour's) if you don't use any chemical sprays. Otherwise, check in your local health food stores. *(See illustration on overleaf facing page 97.)*

INGREDIENTS

Juice of ½ lemon

1 Tbsp/15 mL tahini* (sesame paste) or peanut butter

1 cup/250 mL young organic dandelion leaves,*torn (or watercress)

½ cup/125 mL yoghurt

1 clove garlic

1 cup/250 mL fresh spinach leaves, washed

¼ cup/50 mL chopped nuts or sunflower seeds

Blend the lemon juice, yoghurt, tahini and garlic together in a food processor or blender until smooth. Toss with the dandelion and spinach leaves. Top with chopped nuts or sunflower seeds.

*Available at most organic health food stores.

SERVES 2.

Raw Roots Salad

Jicama comes from Mexico and is similar in appearance to a potato. Peel it and eat raw or cooked. The texture is crisp like a water chestnut. If you can't get jicamas use any other root vegetable, such as parsnip or kholrabi.

INGREDIENTS

1 beetroot, peeled

1 jicama,* peeled or julienned

1 daikon* (large white Oriental radish)

1 turnip, peeled

1 carrot, peeled

Grate or shred the above roots into long spaghetti-type strands and toss with the dressing.

DRESSING

1 tsp/5 mL molasses or honey

3 Tbsp/45 mL olive oil

Cashew nuts, toasted

1 Tbsp/15 mL vinegar

Salt & pepper

Whisk the molasses, vinegar, oil, salt and pepper together in a small bowl and toss with the salad. Sprinkle the finished salad with toasted cashew nuts.

*Available at most organic health food stores and some supermarkets.

SERVES 4 AS A SIDE DISH.

Shrimp & Banana Salad with Lime & Ginger Dressing

INGREDIENTS

2 bananas, peeled & sliced

2 Tbsp/30 mL sake* (or white wine)

1 packet cellophane noodles or
　clear rice vermicelli

Juice of ½ lemon

1 Tbsp/15 mL cornstarch

1 lb/500 g peeled shrimp

Soak the banana slices in lemon juice.

Mix the sake and cornstarch together in a small bowl and toss the shrimp in the mixture. Quickly blanch the shrimp in boiling water, remove and allow to cool.

Cook the noodles for 1 minute in boiling water, turn off the heat and allow to soak for 3 minutes. Drain and cool.

Mix the shrimp, bananas and noodles together and toss with Lime & Ginger Dressing.

LIME & GINGER DRESSING

2 Tbsp/30 mL olive oil

2 Tbsp/30 mL sake*

Zest & juice of ½ orange

1 tsp/5 mL pepper

1 Tbsp/15 mL soy sauce

Zest & juice of ½ lime

1 Tbsp/15 mL grated ginger

Whisk all the above ingredients together in a small bowl and toss with the salad.

*Sake is available at specialty liquor stores.　　　SERVES 4 AS AN APPETIZER.

Carrot Râpé　　　(wrap-**pay**)

INGREDIENTS

2 carrots, grated

½ tsp/2.5 mL salt

1 tsp/5 mL dill

1 tsp/5 mL sesame oil

1 tsp/5 mL black pepper

Juice of ½ orange

1 Tbsp/15 mL parsley, chopped

Mix all the above ingredients together in a large bowl for a refreshing salad.

SERVES 2.

Mexican Salad

An unusual summer salad.

INGREDIENTS

1 beetroot, peeled & sliced

1 orange, peeled & sliced

1 apple, sliced

½ cup/125 mL walnuts, toasted

1 jicama,* peeled & julienned

2 slices pineapple

1 banana, peeled & sliced

2 Tbsp/30 mL pine nuts, toasted

Mix all the fruits and vegetables together in a large salad bowl and toss with Honey Lime Dressing. Arrange on top of lettuce leaves and scatter with walnuts and pine nuts.

HONEY LIME DRESSING

Juice of 1 lime

1 Tbsp/15 mL honey

2 Tbsp/30 mL olive oil

1 clove garlic, finely chopped

1 Tbsp/15 mL vinegar

Pinch salt

Whisk all ingredients together in a small bowl and toss with the fruits and vegetables.

*Available at most organic health food stores and some supermarkets.   SERVES 4.

Tomato, Apple & Yam Salad

INGREDIENTS

*2 yams, boiled, cooled for 30
    minutes, then peeled*

3 Tbsp/45 mL olive oil

Juice of ½ orange

Salt & pepper

Pinch cinnamon

2 apples

2 beefsteak tomatoes

1 Tbsp/15 mL vinegar

1 tsp/5 mL honey

Pinch cloves

3 Tbsp/45 mL chopped pecans, toasted

Slice the yams thickly. Core and slice the apples. Slice the tomatoes. Arrange alternate slices of yams, apples and tomatoes on a platter in overlapping circles.

Mix together the oil, vinegar, orange juice, honey and seasonings and drizzle over the fruit. Sprinkle with chopped toasted pecans.

SERVES 4.

Papaya Dressing

The seeds of the papaya give this dressing a good peppery flavour. It's good on fruit or green salads.

INGREDIENTS

½ papaya

Pinch salt

Juice of ½ lemon

1 Tbsp/15 mL oil

1 Tbsp/15 mL sherry

Seeds of 1 papaya

Scoop out the flesh and seeds of half a papaya and blend with the rest of the ingredients in a food processor or blender until smooth. Use as a dressing over salads or fruits or as a marinade for meats. Keeps for 1 week, refrigerated.

MAKES 1 CUP/250 ML

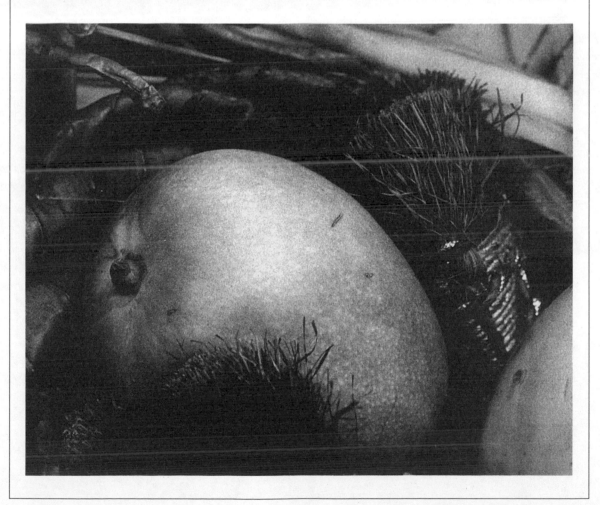

Banana & Pepper Salad

Banana gives this light salad substance.

INGREDIENTS

1 banana, peeled & chopped

½ cup/125 mL chopped parsley

1 Tbsp/15 mL vinegar

2 bell peppers (red, yellow or green)

½ red bell pepper, chopped

2 Tbsp/30 mL olive oil

1 tsp/5 mL sugar

Mix together the banana, red pepper and parsley and toss with the oil, vinegar and sugar. Cut a slice off the top of each pepper and hollow out the insides. Pile the banana mixture into each one and serve.

SERVES 2.

Fresh Strawberry Vegetable Salad

Strawberries are a lovely visual and taste surprise in a vegetable salad. *(See illustration on overleaf facing page 97.)*

INGREDIENTS

1 bunch asparagus, stringy
   ends removed

2 avocados, peeled & sliced

Fresh basil leaves

1 Tbsp/15 mL olive oil

½ cup/125 mL fresh peas

2 cups/500 mL strawberries

1 orange, peeled & sliced

Juice of 1 lemon

Freshly ground black pepper

Cook the asparagus in boiling salted water for 3 to 4 minutes, remove and plunge into cold water. Drain.

Cook the peas in boiling salted water for 2 minutes and drain.

Arrange the strawberries, asparagus, peas, avocados, orange slices and fresh basil leaves on a plate. Drizzle with lemon juice, olive oil and freshly ground black pepper, and serve.

SERVES 4.

> **Although technically a fruit and chemically more like a nut, avocados are commonly considered a vegetable.**

Sides

Everybody likes a little bit on the side. Something sweet, something spicy, something dainty or something strong. Some like it on top, some like it on the bottom, but admit it: everybody likes it some way. ■ Sauces and relishes and other little pretty things are for people who like to play around, people who want just a little something extra to liven up the ordinary. The beauty of them is that you can mix and match and indulge every craving for variety that you ever had, and you'll never end up in divorce court. With a little creativity you can even share them with your spouse. . . . ■

Cačik

(**ca**-chick)

This is a very refreshing condiment. Leave out the garlic if you don't want it to linger.

INGREDIENTS

1 cup/250 mL yoghurt

1 tsp/5 mL vinegar

2 Tbsp/30 mL olive oil

Fresh mint leaves

1 tsp/5 mL salt

1 clove garlic, finely chopped

½ cucumber, peeled & grated

Beat the yoghurt with salt, vinegar, garlic and oil. Stir in the cucumber and chopped mint leaves. Chill. Good with eggplant, lamb kebabs, broad beans or almost anything.

Cayenne Aioli

(**i**-o-lee)

Aioli is really mayonnaise with a good kick to it. It's great with grilled fish.

INGREDIENTS

1 Tbsp/15 mL Dijon mustard

1 Tbsp/15 mL lemon juice

2 egg yolks

2 cloves garlic, finely chopped

Mix the above ingredients together then, pouring slowly, whisk in:

1½ cups/375 mL oil

Salt & pepper

2 Tbsp/30 mL cayenne pepper

Mayonnaise Verde

Mayonnaise Verde is so versatile. Try it on asparagus, or chicken, or fish or even as a base for salad dressing.

INGREDIENTS

1 cup/250 mL mayonnaise

¼ cup/50 mL fresh spinach

1 Tbsp/15 mL pistachio nuts, chopped

½ cup/125 mL parsley, chopped

Few fresh mint leaves

Salt & pepper

Blend all the above ingredients until smooth and creamy.

Salsa Verde

Salsa comes in so many shapes and sizes. Salsa Verde is fresh, light and pretty healthy. Good hot or cold on pasta or as a dip. The perfect food.

INGREDIENTS

½ cup/125 mL parsley, chopped

2 cloves garlic

2 Tbsp/30 mL capers

Juice of ½ lemon

1 hard-boiled egg

2 Tbsp/30 mL mint, chopped

¼ cup/50 mL walnuts, toasted

½ can (3½ oz/100 mL)anchovies

¼ cup/50 mL olive oil

Salt & pepper

Mix all the above ingredients together in a food processor and blend into a thick paste. Serve on hot pasta.

Alternatively, add ½ cup/125 mL pitted black olives to the above salsa and blend further to make an "almost tapenade." Serve with chips or raw vegetables.

Salsa de Almendra Roja   (ahl-**men**-dra **roe**-ha)

Another salsa twist: red almond.

INGREDIENTS

1 slice toast

½ onion, chopped

1 tomato, chopped

½ tsp/2.5 mL ground cumin

Salt & pepper

Juice of ½ lemon

2 Tbsp/30 mL oil

½ cup/125 mL almonds

½ tsp/2.5 mL chili powder

½ tsp/2.5 mL oregano

1 cup/250 mL stock or apple juice

Heat the oil and sauté the onion, almonds, tomato and seasonings until the onion has softened. Blend in a food processor or blender with the rest of the ingredients, including the toast, until smooth. Serve with chicken, any green vegetable or fish.

Raspberry Dip

Blend frozen raspberries with 2 Tbsp/30 mL brandy and 2 Tbsp/30 mL cottage cheese. Serve with freshly sliced fruits.

Rhubarb Relish

A delightful accompaniment to lamb.

INGREDIENTS

½ lb/250 g rhubarb, sliced
Handful of raisins
1 Tbsp/15 mL water
1 tsp/5 mL curry powder
3 Tbsp/45 mL cider vinegar

Handful of chopped dates
½ onion, chopped
3 Tbsp/45 mL brown sugar
½ tsp/2.5 mL cinnamon

Heat all the ingredients in a saucepan, bring to a boil and simmer until the rhubarb has softened. Serve hot or cold with lamb.

Cranberry Sauce

Turkey without cranberry is like a kiss without a squeeze.

INGREDIENTS

1 small can cranberry jelly
Freshly ground black pepper

Zest & juice of ½ orange

Heat the cranberry jelly in a saucepan and stir in the orange zest, orange juice and pepper. Serve with roast turkey.

Prik Dong

Add this Thai chili sauce to stir-fries or use as a dipping sauce. (See illustration on overleaf facing page 128.)

INGREDIENTS

1 cup/250 mL fresh red chili peppers,
    roasted (if using dry, soak
    in vinegar for ½ hour)
⅓ cup/80 mL sake
    (or sweet white wine)

½ cup/125 mL rice vinegar
3 Tbsp/45 mL sugar
1 tsp/5 mL salt
8–9 garlic cloves, whole

Blend in food processor or blender until a coarse paste. Pour into a jar and keep in the fridge.

Flower/Herb Vinegar

Lovely, lovely gifts. *(See illustration on overleaf facing page 128.)*

Fill a clean jar with sprigs of rosemary, juniper berries, chili peppers and pink peppercorns. Pour over these white wine vinegar, leaving ½ in/1 cm head space. Seal and place on a sunny windowsill for 3 weeks.

Strain, reserving the liquid, then place some fresh herbs or flowers in an attractive arrangement in jar and fill with the flavoured vinegar.

Use thyme, lavender, oregano, nasturtiums, chive flowers, marigold, lovage, borage, roses or any combinations that you like.

Banana Chutney

A great accompaniment to curries, pork, chicken or whatever.

INGREDIENTS

⅓ cup/80 mL vinegar
2 bananas, peeled & sliced
1 tsp/5 mL cayenne pepper

2 Tbsp/30 mL sugar
3 green onions, chopped
1 chili pepper, finely chopped

Boil the vinegar and sugar until the sugar has dissolved. Add the rest of the ingredients, simmer for 5 minutes, stirring well, and serve hot or cold.

Mango Chutney

Use on breaded cutlets, or with any curries or any meat dishes you fancy. *(See illustration on overleaf facing page 128.)*

INGREDIENTS

1 Tbsp/15 mL oil
1 clove garlic, finely chopped
3 slices ginger, finely chopped
1 tsp/5 mL vinegar

3 whole red chili peppers
½ onion, finely chopped
1 Tbsp/15 mL sugar
1 mango, peeled & chopped

Heat the oil and add the chili peppers. Stir in the garlic, onion and ginger. Add the sugar and vinegar and, when bubbling, stir in the mango. Cook until thick and syrupy. Serve hot or cold.

Quick Breads

All over the world there are people who will tell you they can't bake bread. What they really mean is that they can't bake bread the way their mothers or grandmothers did. Mamma worked at it for hours, and what emerged from the oven was more than bread. She opened the oven door and lifted out an art form that was an original and unwritten recipe—a mixture of equal parts of culture, mythology and love, all seasoned with her secret ingredient: Time. ■ Today's Mammas have joined the rest of us in a world where Time just doesn't grow in the fields any more. Ask for Time in a store and the clerks shake their heads sadly and they all tell you the same thing: "Oh no, we don't sell *that,* nobody makes it any more." ■ Now, about these people who can't bake bread. What they really need to know is that Mamma didn't always spend hours making bread. She too had her moments of panic, when she needed something fresh, and quick, and simple, because somebody was coming to supper and sliced bread just wasn't good enough. She made bannock and scones and cornbread and muffins. Sometimes she did it on the tailgate of a wagon and sometimes in a woodstove with an oven. Downtown or on the farm, anybody can make quick breads, in less time than it takes to figure out how your fancy new watch works. Twenty minutes from beginning there's a smell coming out of the oven, and you're three-quarters along the road to having a reputation. Breakfast, lunch, supper—the next time someone tells you that they would love to bake but they just don't have the time, simply smile and invite them over for some home-made muffins. Mamma would be proud. ■

Chapatis

INGREDIENTS

1 cup/250 mL whole wheat flour
7–8 Tbsp/100–120 mL cold
    water (approx.)

½ tsp/2.5 mL salt

Sift the flour and salt into a mixing bowl. Slowly add the water (adding more or less than indicated) to make a smooth, elastic dough. Knead quickly and allow to stand for about 30 minutes.

Taking small handfuls, roll each one in the palm of your hand to make a ball. Flatten out on a floured board and roll out to a thin round. Make it quick and light.

Heat a dry frypan and fry over medium-high until light brown on both sides. Remove from the pan. If you have a gas stovetop, take a pair of tongs and hold each side of the chapati over the open flame (for a few seconds only) so that each side puffs up.

Stack on a plate covered with a cloth. You can then brush them with a little butter and serve warm with the meal.

MAKES 4.

Flower Pot Bread

A wonderful and unusual hostess present. *(See illustration facing page 128.)*

INGREDIENTS

2½ cups/625 mL whole wheat flour
1 Tbsp/15 mL baking powder
2 Tbsp/30 mL brown sugar
1–1¼ cups/250–300 mL yoghurt

½ tsp/2.5 mL salt
1 egg
¼ cup/50 mL vegetable oil

Preheat the oven to 400°F/200°C.

Grease and line a medium-sized clay flower pot with parchment paper (or use 3 small clay flower pots). Sift the flour, salt and baking powder into a mixing bowl. Beat in the egg, sugar, oil and yoghurt and tip the dough into the flower pot. Bake for 35 to 45 minutes or until it sounds hollow when tapped.

MAKES 1 LOAF OR 3 SMALL LOAVES.

Prune & Peach Hot Biscuits

INGREDIENTS

½ cup/125 mL dried pitted prunes

1 cup/250 mL flour

½ tsp/2.5 mL salt

1 can (14 oz/398 mL) peach halves

5 Tbsp/75 mL hot water

2 tsp/10 mL baking powder

6 Tbsp/90 mL milk

Preheat the oven to 400°F/200°C.

Blend the prunes and hot water to a coarse consistency in a food processor. Sift in the flour, baking powder and salt and pour in the milk (adding a little more if necessary) until it comes away in a ball.

Remove from the bowl onto a floured board and pat out to a ½-in/1-cm thickness. Using a pastry cutter or glass or free-hand, cut out shapes.

Pour the peach halves and juice into a baking dish and place the pastry shapes on top. Bake for 15 minutes.

SERVES 4.

Griddle Cakes

A Sunday morning classic!

INGREDIENTS

½ cup/125 mL flour

½ tsp/2.5 mL salt

1½ cups/375 mL cooked oatmeal

¼ cup/50 mL water

1 tsp/5 mL baking powder

1 egg

½ cup/125 mL evaporated milk

2 Tbsp/30 mL melted butter

Sift the flour, baking powder and salt into a mixing bowl. In another bowl, beat the egg and stir in the rest of the ingredients. Pour this mixture into the dry ingredients.

Gently pour spoonfuls onto a hot griddle pan or large frypan and cook over medium heat on the first side until the batter bubbles. Flip and cook until light brown on the other side.

Serve with yoghurt and fresh strawberries and drizzle with maple syrup.

SERVES 4.

Coconut Muffins

Just a hint of coconut.

INGREDIENTS

3 Tbsp/45 mL grated coconut
1 Tbsp/15 mL baking powder
2 Tbsp/30 mL butter
2 eggs

1 cup/250 mL flour
3 Tbsp/45 mL raisins
2 Tbsp/30 mL sugar
1 tsp/5 mL vanilla

Preheat oven to 350°F/180°C.

Soak the coconut in a little hot water for 5 minutes to soften. Drain. Mix the flour, baking powder and raisins in a bowl. In another bowl cream the butter, sugar and coconut together and beat in the eggs and vanilla.

Fold the flour mixture into the coconut mixture and spoon into small greased muffin tins. Dust with sugar and bake for 15 minutes.

MAKES 6.

Quick Coffee Muffins

A quick morning pick-me-up!

INGREDIENTS

1½ cups/375 mL flour
¼ tsp/1 mL salt
½ cup/125 mL sugar
2 eggs

1½ tsp/7.5 mL baking powder
1 Tbsp/15 mL instant coffee
1 cup/250 mL sour cream (or thick yoghurt)

Preheat oven to 350°F/180°C.

Sift the flour, baking powder, salt, coffee and sugar into a mixing bowl. In another bowl beat the sour cream and eggs together and pour into the dry ingredients.

Mix lightly and pour into greased muffin tins. Bake for 10 to 15 minutes.

MAKES 6 LARGE MUFFINS.

Desserts

You don't always have to serve dessert. Sometimes it's nice to sit back and let the spicy dinner flavours float around in your mouth, and not swamp them with sugar. Because that's what sugar does, it wipes out a lot of taste. In Thailand, where food is sometimes too hot even for the Thai palates, there is frequently a little bowl of palm sugar on the table, and it's the most effective antidote there is for too much hot chili pepper. Sugar is one of those ingredients that takes over from everything else. ■ But the trick for successful desserts is to keep them in their place. I watch people racing through their dinners and, as they say, "saving themselves for dessert." Everything that comes before the final sugar hit is ignored in favour of whipped cream and chocolate, and you, if you're the cook, quietly wonder if all those nice things you did with the lamb chops or the chicken were really worthwhile. ■ Dessert is really a habit, but it doesn't have to be a bad habit. Cravings are natural and in some cases even good for you. Feed them well, and then, ever so gently, feed them something delicate, and pretty, and sweet, and remember that dessert is not the beginning or end of life, just a wonderful way to finish an equally wonderful meal, and some meals are best savoured with-

out it. ■ Sometimes the best way to eat sweets is all by themselves— chocolate chip cookies on a rainy Sunday, ice cream with applesauce in the middle of a long night. Anything in moderation. Eat them with joy, stop before you're full, and walk away guilt-free and happy. ■

Shortbread & Whiskey

I think shortbreads should be eaten year-round—particularly these ones.

INGREDIENTS

  6 Tbsp/90 mL butter   3 Tbsp/45 mL sugar
  1 Tbsp/15 mL semolina   ⅓ cup/80 mL flour

Preheat oven to 350°F/180°C.

Cream the butter and sugar in a food processor. Add the semolina and then the flour. Remove and knead quickly. Press into a tin, prick the top with a fork and bake for 20 to 25 minutes. Cool in the tin.

Mix 1 tsp/5 mL whiskey with 1 cup/250 mL whipped cream. Cut shortbread into wedges and serve with whipped cream.

SERVES 2.

Huevos Reales   (**hway**-vose ray-**el**-ays)

Royal Eggs. Well named.

INGREDIENTS

  2 egg yolks   8 egg whites
  1 cup/250 mL sugar   3 cloves
  ½ cup/125 mL water   1 stick cinnamon
  ⅓ cup/80 mL raisins   ½ cup/125 mL slivered almonds
    soaked in rum or brandy

Preheat oven to 350°F/180°C. Grease and line an 8-in/20-cm cake tin.

Beat the egg yolks. Beat egg whites stiffly and fold into egg yolks. Pour into the tin and place in a baking dish with enough water to come halfway up. Bake for 15 to 20 minutes and allow to cool in the tin.

Meanwhile, heat the sugar, cloves, water and cinnamon, bring to a boil and cook for 2 minutes. Remove cloves and cinnamon.

Cut the cake into wedges, place on a plate, pour the sauce over the top and allow to stand. Sprinkle with the almonds and drained raisins.

SERVES 4.

Banana French Toast

Too good to restrict to breakfast.

⅓ cup/80 mL chopped walnuts

1 banana, peeled

2 slices raisin bread or 2 stale
   croissants, halved

¼ tsp/1 mL cinnamon

2 Tbsp/30 mL butter

1 tsp/5 mL butter

1 Tbsp/15 mL orange juice

1 Tbsp/15 mL rum, optional

3 eggs

½ cup/125 mL milk

Lightly sauté the walnuts in 1 tsp/5 mL butter until hot and set aside.

Mash the banana and mix with the orange juice. Spread the mixture on a slice of bread and make a sandwich. Mix the rest of the ingredients together, except the butter, and soak the bread in this for a few seconds.

Melt the butter and fry the sandwich on both sides until golden brown. Sprinkle the chopped walnuts on top and serve with cream or yoghurt.

SERVES 2.

Jamaican Hot Fruit Salad

This one is a show stopper. It's terrific over ice cream or just on its own.

2 14-oz/398-mL cans peaches

3 Tbsp/45 mL brown sugar

4 bananas, sliced

6 Tbsp/90 mL dark rum

Chop all the fruit and mix with half of the juice from the cans. Heat in a saucepan with the sugar until boiling and cook for 5 minutes. Stir in the rum and set light to the salad. Serve immediately.

As an alternative, cook this dish in the oven while everyone is eating their main course. Preheat the oven to 500°F/250°C. Mix all the fruits, sugar and rum together in a baking dish. Put fruit on the top shelf of the oven and let cook furiously for 10 minutes. Remove from the oven. Heat a ladleful of rum to boiling, light and pour it flaming over the fruit salad.

SERVES 4.

Toot (Marzipan Shapes)

Some fun for the kids. If you don't want to make the paste yourself, buy it ready-made.

INGREDIENTS

¼ cup/50 mL ground almonds

¼ cup/50 mL icing sugar

5 Tbsp/75 mL castor sugar or
 superfine sugar

½ tsp/2.5 mL ground cardamom

2 Tbsp/30 mL rosewater

Pistachio slivers

Mix the ground almonds, cardamom, icing sugar and rosewater together and knead into a paste. Take small pieces and mould into shapes (e.g. berries), roll in castor sugar and decorate with pistachio slivers.

Carrot Cake

An all-time favourite. I sometimes substitute raisins for the pineapple.

INGREDIENTS

1 cup/250 mL flour

1 Tbsp/15 mL baking powder

½ cup/125 mL vegetable oil

½ cup/125 mL walnuts, chopped

1 tsp/5 mL ground cinnamon

¼ tsp/1 mL salt

2 eggs

1 cup/250 mL carrots, grated

½ cup/125 mL grated coconut

1 small can crushed pineapple, drained

Preheat oven to 350°F/180°C.

Sift the flour, salt and baking powder together. Beat the eggs and oil and stir into the flour. Add the carrots, walnuts, coconut, pineapple and cinnamon, mix well and pour into greased muffin tins or loaf tins.

Bake for 25 to 30 minutes, or until tester comes out clean. Cool before icing.

CREAM CHEESE ICING

2 Tbsp/30 mL butter

1 cup/250 mL icing sugar, sifted

Juice of ½ orange or lemon

3 Tbsp/45 mL cream cheese

½ tsp/2.5 mL vanilla

Cream the butter and cream cheese and sift in the icing sugar. Add vanilla and juice. Spread over the cooled loaf or muffins.

MAKES 1 LOAF OR 6 LARGE MUFFINS.

Rose Petal Fruit Salad

For very special occasions.

INGREDIENTS

2 cups/500 mL strawberries, sliced

2 kiwis, sliced

1 tsp/5 mL sugar

1 cup/250 mL mango, sliced

½ cup/125 mL Grand Marnier or orange juice

2 red roses, untreated

Allow the fruit, Grand Marnier or orange juice and sugar to steep for 30 minutes. Pour into a glass bowl and decorate with rose petals.

SERVES 4.

Ice Cream & Hot Marmalade Sauce

The bite of the hot marmalade and brandy is a nice contrast to the cold and creamy ice cream.

INGREDIENTS

3 Tbsp/45 mL ginger marmalade
 or other marmalade of
 your choice

1 glass brandy

Zest of a lemon

Ice cream

Boil the marmalade, brandy and zest until thickened and pour over the ice cream.

TOPPING FOR 4.

Sooji Halva

A sweet Indian pudding. Soothing, but not to everyone's taste.

INGREDIENTS

1½ Tbsp/22 mL butter

1 cup/250 mL water or milk

¼ cup/50 mL sugar (jaggery)

½ cup/125 mL semolina (sooji)

½ cup/125 mL cashew nuts, chopped

6 green cardamoms

Melt the butter in a frypan and add the semolina. Stir well until slightly brown. Pour in the water or milk and stir. Add the nuts and sugar and continue stirring. Turn off the heat and add the seeds of 6 green cardamoms. Serve decorated with dried rose petals.

SERVES 4.

French Strawberry Tart

A great summer brunch dish and very pretty on the table.

INGREDIENTS

1 packet frozen puff pastry

Juice of ½ lemon

1 beaten egg

2 cups/500 mL sliced strawberries

1 Tbsp/15 mL sugar

2 Tbsp/30 mL apricot jam

Preheat oven to 400°F/200°C.

Roll out the pastry to make a rectangle. Prick all over. Arrange sliced strawberries on top. Sprinkle with lemon juice and sugar. Brush the pastry border with beaten egg and bake for 15 minutes.

Heat the jam in a saucepan, remove the cooked tart, allow to cool a little and pour or brush the warm jam over the top to glaze. Eat with whipped cream.

SERVES 4.

Zabaglione

(za-**ba**-lee-o-nee)

Most of us have witnessed the drama of zabaglione preparation; an officious waiter invariably makes it appear that a certain expertise is absolutely essential for success. But it's much easier than pie.

INGREDIENTS

1 egg	*1 tsp/5 mL sugar*
1 Tbsp/15 mL sherry	*1 Tbsp/15 mL cream*

Beat the egg, sugar, sherry and cream until pale. Steam in a cappuccino/milk steamer or pour mixture in a ramekin and place in frypan with enough boiling water to come halfway up the sides of the ramekin dish. Or put mixture in the top of a double boiler and whisk away.

In any case, steam until the mixture swells into a thick foam. Serve in a warm glass.

SERVES 1.

Instant Vegetarian Mincemeat

I never seem to have thought far enough in advance to have the mincemeat made and put away for the festive season. This one solves that problem—and it's much lighter than the original meat-and-suet version.

INGREDIENTS

1 Tbsp/15 mL butter	*4 slices bread, cubed*
4 dried figs, chopped	*½ cup/125 mL sultanas*
6 pitted prunes, chopped	*½ glass rum*
5 apples, cored, peeled & diced	*½ tsp/2.5 mL cloves*
½ tsp/2.5 mL nutmeg	*½ tsp/2.5 mL cinnamon*
½ cup/125 mL brown sugar	

Melt the butter and lightly fry the bread. Stir in the dried figs, sultanas and prunes and pour in the rum. Stir everything until the rum is absorbed. Add the apples together with the cloves, nutmeg, cinnamon and brown sugar and mix well.

Put in vol-au-vents, or stuff apples with the mixture, or use wherever mincemeat is called for.

Rose Crèpes

A Valentine's Day natural.

CREPES

  3 eggs

  6 Tbsp/90 mL flour

  1 cup/250 mL milk

  Pinch salt

FILLING

  Handful of organic rose petals

  Freshly ground black pepper

  Icing sugar

  2 cups/500 mL strawberries

  Rosewater

Blend the crepe ingredients and let stand for 30 minutes.

Brush a frypan with a little butter and pour in 3 Tbsp/45 mL batter, tilting the pan so that batter spreads evenly over the pan. Flip the crepe over and lightly brown the other side, about 20 seconds.

Stuff each crepe with fresh organic rose petals, fresh strawberries (half sliced and half partially crushed) and sprinkle with black pepper and rosewater. Dust with icing sugar and serve.

SERVES 2.

No-Bake Chocolate Cake

For those of us who need that fix. *(See illustration facing page 129.)*

INGREDIENTS

  6 Tbsp/90 mL butter

  10–12 digestive biscuits (crushed
    in waxed paper or plastic
    bag with rolling pin)

  2 oz/56 g baker's chocolate (2 squares)

  ½ cup/125 mL roasted, chopped pecans

  ½ cup/125 mL dried, chopped figs

Grease a 9-in/23-cm springform pan. Melt the butter and chocolate over low heat. Stir in the biscuit crumbs, pecans and figs and press into the cake tin. Chill overnight.

SERVES 6.

> **You can save 100 calories every time you substitute 2 tsp of cocoa for each square of unsweetened chocolate in a recipe.**

Chocolate Chip Cookies

The oatmeal adds a nutty flavour to complement the walnuts. Raisins are a nice addition too.

INGREDIENTS

½ cup/125 mL butter

2 eggs

1 cup/250 mL flour

½ tsp/2.5 mL baking powder

½ cup/125 mL chocolate chips

½ cup/125 mL rolled oats

½ cup/125 mL brown sugar

½ tsp/2.5 mL vanilla

½ tsp/2.5 mL baking soda

½ tsp/2.5 mL salt

½ cup/125 mL walnuts, chopped

Preheat oven to 350°F/180°C.

Cream the butter and sugar and beat in the eggs and vanilla. Sift the flour, baking soda, baking powder and salt together and add to the butter mixture. Fold in the chocolate chips, nuts and oats.

Drop teaspoonfuls onto a greased cookie sheet and bake for 15 minutes or until browned.

MAKES AS FEW AS 4 AND AS MANY AS 24 (depending on the size you like them).

Toffee Water Chestnuts

An unusual combination.

INGREDIENTS

½ lb/250 g fresh water chestnuts, washed & scraped, or 1 can

2 Tbsp/30 mL sugar

2 Tbsp/30 mL hot water

6 bamboo skewers

1 Tbsp/15 mL oil

2 Tbsp/30 mL syrup

Thread water chestnuts onto each skewer. Heat the oil in a frypan and bring the sugar, syrup and water to the boil. Stir until caramelized. Add the skewers and turn until covered with syrup. Serve hot or cold.

SERVES 6.

> **The Aztecs of Mexico believed that cacao beans were seeds from paradise.**

Coffee Dessert

Pretty close to Tiramisu but not quite as rich (or as expensive to make).

INGREDIENTS

2 Tbsp/30 mL butter

2 Tbsp/30 mL sugar

2 Tbsp/30 mL rum

2 Tbsp/30 mL cream cheese

1 egg white, beaten

1 Tbsp/15 mL flour

1 cup/250 mL strong coffee

6 sponge fingers

2 Tbsp/30 mL whipped cream

1 Tbsp/15 mL cocoa powder

Melt the butter in a saucepan. Mix the flour and sugar and stir into the butter. Add the coffee and rum and bring to the boil, stirring all the time. Lay the sponge fingers in a glass bowl and pour the coffee sauce over the fingers. Cool.

Mix the cream cheese, whipped cream and egg white together and pour on top of the sauce. Sprinkle with cocoa powder and serve cold.

SERVES 2.

Avocado & Coffee Ice Cream

I continue to include a recipe for avocado ice cream in my cookbooks, hoping that one of these days a few of you might try it. You'll either really like it or you won't. I think it's great.

INGREDIENTS

2 avocados, mashed

1 tsp/5 mL lemon juice

1 cup/250 mL whipped cream

1 tsp/5 mL instant coffee

1 tsp/5 mL sugar

Mix together and freeze.

SERVES 2.

Tomato Soup Cake

Carrot cake, zucchini bread, why not tomato soup cake?

INGREDIENTS

⅓ cup/80 mL butter, soft

1½ cups/375 mL flour

1 tsp/5 mL baking powder

1 tsp/5 mL cinnamon

1 12-oz/340-mL can tomato soup

½ cup/125 mL sugar

1 tsp/5 mL baking soda

½ tsp/2.5 mL ground cloves

1 egg

1 cup/250 mL raisins

Preheat oven to 350°F/180°C.

Cream the butter and sugar. Sift dry ingredients together and add to butter mixture. Beat in the egg and soup. Stir in the raisins and pour into a small loaf tin. Bake for 25 to 30 minutes.

YIELDS 1 SMALL LOAF.

Chocolate Krispies

Kids adore this stuff.

INGREDIENTS

3 Tbsp/45 mL butter

2 Tbsp/30 mL cocoa powder

2 Tbsp/30 mL golden syrup

1 cup/250 mL Rice Krispies

Melt the butter, syrup and cocoa powder and pour into a bowl with the Rice Krispies. Stir and spoon into paper muffin cases. Chill.

Baked Alaska

This became a classic because it's so easy to make.

INGREDIENTS

1 sponge cake, cut into 2 layers   *2 cups/500 mL ice cream*

3 egg whites   *Pinch salt*

¼ tsp/1 mL cream of tartar   *3 Tbsp/45 mL icing sugar*

Preheat oven to 500°F/250°C.

Working quickly, spoon ice cream onto 1 layer of the sponge cake (making it a little narrower than the cake) and cover with the second layer.

Beat the egg whites, salt and cream of tartar until frothy, then beat in the sugar until stiff. Cover the sponge with meringue and bake for 5 minutes. Serve immediately.

Chocolate Sandwiches

Ridiculously simple.

INGREDIENTS

Grated chocolate   *4 slices bread*

2 Tbsp/30 mL oil or butter   *1 egg, beaten*

Sprinkle a good layer of grated chocolate over 2 of the slices of bread. Cover with the other 2 slices. Heat the oil or butter in a frypan, dip the sandwiches in the beaten egg and fry until golden brown. Cut into triangles and serve.

SERVES 2.

Chocolate-Dipped Grapes

These are really beautiful. Try making half with white chocolate using purple grapes and the other half with dark chocolate and green grapes. *(See illustration facing page 129.)*

Melt 1 bar of semisweet chocolate in a double saucepan and dip small bunches of grapes in the hot chocolate. Lay on parchment paper and chill in the refrigerator until serving.

Banana & Coconut

INGREDIENTS

3 bananas
1 Tbsp/15 mL flour
1 Tbsp/15 mL butter

1 cup/250 mL grated coconut
1 Tbsp/15 mL sugar

Mash the bananas with the coconut, flour and sugar. Form into small balls, roll in more coconut and gently fry in butter until brown.
   Serve with fresh sliced mangoes or any fruit (or puréed raspberries).

SERVES 4.

Thai-Style Rice & Mangoes

A different take on rice puddin'.

INGREDIENTS

1 14-oz/398-mL can coconut milk
¼ tsp/1 mL salt
2 mangoes, peeled

2 Tbsp/30 mL sugar
2 cups/500 mL cooked white rice

Heat the coconut milk, sugar and salt, remove from the heat and stir in the cooked rice. Allow to stand for a few minutes and decorate with sliced mangoes.

SERVES 4.

Baked Bananas with Cheese & Brazil Nuts

This is really very tasty.

INGREDIENTS

½ cup/125 mL Brazil nuts

3 bananas, peeled & sliced lengthwise

4 Tbsp/60 mL cheddar cheese,
    grated (or Parmesan)

2 eggs, beaten

¼ tsp/1 mL grated nutmeg

1 Tbsp/15 mL butter

2 Tbsp/30 mL brown sugar

¼ tsp/1 mL salt

½ cup/125 mL cream

1 tsp/5 mL cinnamon

½ tsp/2.5 mL cayenne pepper

Chop and toast the Brazil nuts. Melt the butter in a frypan, lay the bananas in the pan and sprinkle with brown sugar, salt, nuts and 3 Tbsp/45 mL grated cheese. Beat the cream, eggs, cinnamon and nutmeg together and pour over the top. Sprinkle with 1 Tbsp/15 mL grated cheese and the cayenne pepper.

Cover and cook slowly until set, about 10 to 15 minutes. Serve immediately.

SERVES 4.

Strawberry Whizz

INGREDIENTS

1 cup/250 mL strawberries

1 tsp/5 mL sugar

Black pepper to taste

3 Tbsp/45 mL yoghurt

Pinch of salt

Ice cubes

Blend all the ingredients in a blender and serve as a drink or as a sauce for dessert. Garnish with mint sprigs.

MAKES 1 BEVERAGE.

Beverages

When I first came to Canada I flew pretty well straight up to a construction site in the far (at least that's what they told me it was) far North. It was romantic—I had visions of me in a canoe, trout in all the streams and wild animals looking coy round the back of every tree. I dreamed of a moosehide jacket and hand-embroidered moccasins. There would be dinners by a smoky campfire and (despite being a fairly competent engineer) I somehow thought of me and a couple of other guys spending a couple of hours a day building this dam across the Kemano River, to make a little electricity for the aluminum company. ■ But it wasn't like that at all. There were about 3000 of us, all of us working twelve-, sometimes sixteen-hour days. And we didn't sleep under the stars. We had little rooms in tin huts, two guys to a room, and it seemed that no matter who I got to share a room with he had smelly feet. We didn't get fresh-caught trout for our suppers. We got mostly meat, enormous great slabs of it, four or five pounds each was nothing. It was bitterly cold and we had to keep our internal heating systems working full blast. We ate enormous breakfasts of hotcakes, not just plain hotcakes with maple syrup but great towering structures almost as big as the dam we were building. I watched at my first breakfast as a man put a hotcake on a plate, put two slices of ham on it, then another hotcake and three sausages, another hotcake and two fried eggs, another hotcake and four or five pats of butter and finally, this *is* true, the contents of a can of sardines. Then he poured maple syrup over the lot, and ate it. He wasn't unusual, except for the sardines. ■ We all took Thermos bottles to breakfast and filled them with coffee. The coffee was a major disappointment. It was weak and acidic and always, somehow, muddy. And all the way across the Atlantic, from London to Quebec, we had been told tales of how wonderful the coffee was in Canada. It never ever lived up to the advance billing—Canadian coffee always impressed me by its wimpiness—and it's only a couple of years ago that anything approaching good coffee has been reasonably available in restaurants or most houses. ■ And it's all to do with the cappuccino machines that seem to be selling faster than they can get them off the ships from Italy. There's hardly a village left in Canada, even the traditional Prairie whistle stop, which doesn't have an espresso bar in the shadow of its grain elevator. And the good ol' boys, the ones that I used to work alongside, are all in there slurping down their foam, nibbling on croissants and brioches and those fancy Italian cookies called biscotti. ■ But there's a lot more to a decent cup of coffee than just something lukewarm and brown. The cappuccino bar is taking over from a lot of the other kind of bars, and in doing so it's changing our social habits. You don't get strippers and waitresses in bunny costumes in cappuccino bars, you don't get those

very loud and repetitive conversations, and it seems to me that there are a lot fewer people arguing about who won the Grey Cup in 1634. You don't get fights in cappuccino bars, and you don't get people falling flat on their faces on the way to drive the car home. ■ People read in cappuccino bars, they play chess (at least they do in Vancouver), and there's an awful lot of people I know who seem to breakfast on caffè latte during the week, and on weekends, because they feel at home and comfortable, they take their kids into the same bar for an ice cream. ■ And it's this social aspect of a decent cup of coffee which is most important. Private clubs have membership fees, and if you join one you more or less expect to be around for a while, you're stable and settled down and you're fairly rich. But the people on the way up in life (or the way through) who aren't in that league, they've got somewhere to go that's reasonably comfortable, where the guy behind the counter may not say in that well-oiled private club manner, "Good evening, Sir William, I'll bring your gin and tonic immediately," but he does say "Hi Chuck—got the day off today, eh???" ■ And women can be a lot more comfortable in a cappuccino bar than a booze bar. Admittedly there are elegant bars around, in major hotels, and they're quiet and respectable, but to start off with they're expensive, and a drink (as in "Why don't we have a drink this evening, eh?") always seems to have overtones of unfinished business, like "Why don't we go and have a bite? I know this little place around the corner." Women can sit happily in a cappuccino bar without anybody stumbling over and offering them a latte, without anybody saying, "What's a nice-lookin' girl like you doin' in a place like this?" and it seems to me that cappuccino is one of the more civilizing things that has happened to us in a long time. It'll be a pity if it just turns out to be a yuppie fashion fad. ■

Whiskey Hot Toddy

INGREDIENTS

1–2 Tbsp/15–30 mL whiskey
1 cup/250 mL hot water
Cinnamon stick

1 Tbsp/15 mL honey
Lemon slices

Put the whiskey and honey into a glass mug and pour in the hot water. Stir well and serve with a slice of lemon and a cinnamon stick.

SERVES 1.

Chocolate con Leche

If you like hot chocolate, you'll like this.

INGREDIENTS

2 oz/56 g chocolate (baking
   chocolate or regular is fine)
1/3 cup/80 mL sugar
1/2 tsp/2.5 mL nutmeg
Cinnamon sticks

1/2 cup/125 mL boiling water
4 cups/1 L hot milk
1/2 tsp/2.5 mL cinnamon
1 tsp/5 mL vanilla

Melt the chocolate and water in pan. Pour in the hot milk and sugar and stir in the spices. Whisk well until frothy and pour into mugs. Put a cinnamon stick in each mug and serve.

SERVES 4.

Chai   (chi)

An Asian cure for colds.

INGREDIENTS

1/2 cup/125 mL milk
1 Tbsp/15 mL tea leaves
1/2 tsp/2.5 mL cinnamon

1/2 cup/125 mL water
1/2 tsp/2.5 mL ground ginger
1/2 tsp/2.5 mL ground cardamom

Heat the milk and water in a saucepan. Bring to a boil, lower the heat and add the rest of the ingredients. Simmer for 2 to 3 minutes. Strain and serve.

SERVES 1.

Orange Vodka

The ultimate surreptitious drink!

INGREDIENTS

1 orange per person
Syringe

Vodka

Inject each orange with vodka and suck out the juices!

Rhumba

If you can't do the Rhumba, at least try the drink!

INGREDIENTS

1 Tbsp/15 mL honey
2 Tbsp/30 mL rum
Orange slices

1 cup/250 mL milk
Pinch ground nutmeg

Heat the honey, milk and rum. Bring to a boil and pour into a mug. Sprinkle with nutmeg and garnish with orange slices.

SERVES 1.

Teddy Bear

You'll want to cuddle with Paddington after this one!

INGREDIENTS

1 Earl Grey tea bag
Pinch cinnamon

1 cup/250 mL milk

Steam the milk and pour onto the tea bag in a mug. Remove tea bag when strong enough. Sprinkle with cinnamon and serve with a cinnamon stick.

SERVES 1.

Gossip's Cup

Moderation is the key or this drink may well live up to its name.

INGREDIENTS

2 bottles ale

1 Tbsp/15 mL brown sugar

Pinch nutmeg

1 Tbsp/15 mL brandy

1 slice lemon peel

Pinch ginger

Mix ingredients in a saucepan. Heat but don't boil and pour into glasses. Serve with a large cinnamon stick to stir.

SERVES 2.

Raspberry Vodka

Absolutely colourful! *(See illustration on overleaf facing page 129.)*

INGREDIENTS

2 cups/500 mL fresh raspberries, crushed,
    or frozen

½ cup/125 mL sugar

Vodka

Take a clean 20-oz/500-mL bottle with screw top. Fill with the raspberries, add the sugar and top up with vodka. Cap and shake once a day until the sugar dissolves (4 to 5 days). Wait, if you can, for 2 months and decant.

> **Raspberries are best not washed.**
>
> **After all, one must have faith in**
>
> **something.**

Chocolate Drink

INGREDIENTS

1 cup/250 mL milk

Grated chocolate

1 Tbsp/15 mL maple syrup

Heat the milk and whisk in the maple syrup. Top with grated chocolate and serve in a mug.

SERVES 1.

Pineapple Smoothie

Close your eyes and think of the pool side.

INGREDIENTS

2 Tbsp/30 mL coconut milk

Juice of ½ lemon

Ice

1 can pineapple juice (8–12 oz/227–340 mL)

1 Tbsp/15 mL rum

Put all ingredients in a blender and whizz until smooth. Serve chilled.

SERVES 1.

Banana Smoothie

INGREDIENTS

1 banana

Scoop of ice cream

Milk (depending
  on desired thickness)

2 Tbsp/30 mL brandy, optional

Whizz everything together in a blender and serve in a glass.

SERVES 1.

Index

Recipe titles are in *italic;* main ingredients or types
of food are in roman type.